PAUL
MARTIN'S
BRITAIN

PAUL MARTIN'S BRITAIN

PAUL MARTIN

SUTTON PUBLISHING

First published in the United Kingdom in 2007 by
Sutton Publishing · Cirencester Road · Chalford ·
Stroud · Gloucestershire · GL6 8PE

British Library Cataloguing in Publication Data
A catalogue record for this book is available from
the British Library.

Hardback ISBN 978-0-7509-4725-1
Paperback ISBN 978-0-7509-4726-8

Typeset in 11½/16pt Berkley Old Style.
Designed by Glad Stockdale.
Typesetting and origination by
Sutton Publishing Limited.
Printed and bound in England.

I would like to dedicate this book to my
mum, Tess, and my wife, Charlotte.

Contents

1. Seeing off the Competition   1

2. Drum Beats   7

3. Finding a Style   19

4. In Praise of Brown Leaves   25

5. Position in the Provinces   31

6. In the Right Place at the Right Time   37

7. New Boy in the Class   41

8. Turning a Profit   49

9. How *Flog It!* Works   55

10. Civic Pride   63

11. Missing the Mark   69

12. Going, Going, Gone   77

13. Bluebell Blues   87

14. So Many Strange Beds   91

15. Hurrah for the National Trust   97

16. Pictures of Britain   101

17. Seeing Sculpture   115

18. Working with Wood   121

19. Pottering around the Lake District   127

20. Wales, my Spiritual Home   131

21. A Trip to Northern Ireland   137

22. One Man, One City, One Mighty Scotsman   145

23. Fabulous Furniture   149

24. Great Gardening   157

25. Beach Combing   167

26. Travelling through Time   173

27. Tracking Isambard   179

28. Man-Made Motors   187

29. Treasuring Trams   195

30. Road Rules   199

31. In Fine Fettle   203

32. Bonkers   213

33. Sunset Skills   223

34. What Would You Do, Paul?   231

35. Being James May   235

36. The Beat Lives on   241

Picture Credits   248

Acknowledgements   248

1

Seeing off the Competition

'You're up against *SpongeBob SquarePants*,' announced a grim-faced executive at the BBC's Whiteladies Road offices at the start of a strategy meeting.

'I'm what?'

'That's what ITV is screening,' he explained, a copy of the *TV Times* on his lap.

'Spongy . . . Pants?' I looked puzzled. I was puzzled.

'You know,' another senior producer assured me.

I didn't.

'CITV,' a third exec added.

All four of them nodded.

They all knew what I was up against. I felt guilty about my ignorance.

Paul Martin's Britain

'He's going to take 30 per cent-plus of the available audience.'

'Who is he?' I said.

'A cartoon character on ITV. They've put his new series up against us at 3.45.'

Ah, I was starting to get it. The man in the spongy pants would be on ITV at the same time as *Flog It!* was showing on BBC2.

'It's fifteen minutes into *Countdown*.'

Was this good or bad?

'They don't like Des.'

'He's doing all right.'

'Des doesn't like it.'

'If he pulls out, they might let Carol Vorderman do it.'

'She won't be right.'

'Then *Deal or No Deal* starts at 4.15.'

'They won't come over at 4.15.'

'You'll be halfway through the second part of the valuation day.'

'They won't know what you're talking about, and they won't care.'

'They won't know where you are, and there's no jeopardy.'

'They'll go straight from *Countdown* to Noel Edmonds.'

'Can we put some jeopardy in two-thirds of the way through?'

There were a few seconds of silence while the executives contemplated this possibility.

The landscape of late afternoon telly had become an ugly battlefield by the autumn of 2006.

Paul O'Grady and numbers in boxes were to blame.

A year ago everyone knew how the land lay. There were kids' shows on BBC1 and ITV, Channel 4 had *Countdown*, Five had old films and BBC2 had *Ready, Steady, Cook*, *The Weakest Link* and *Flog It!* The available audience knew what was what, and where and when it was happening.

Then a whole lot of things happened. Richard Whiteley died and Des Lynam took his place. ITV decided there were better

What follows *Flog It!*?
Ready, Steady, Cook.

viewing figures and advertising revenue to be had from running a general entertainment show rather than children's fare at 5 p.m., so they persuaded Paul O'Grady to do a sort of extended pantomime act in front of a studio audience, which seemed to work well. It was like a Saturday morning kids' show, but nominally aimed at grown-ups.

Then Channel 4 discovered the magical appeal of people guessing whether one box had more money in it than another, with Noel Edmonds lurking around the decision-makers as if they were about to determine the best way to split the atom.

One lesson that seemed to be learned from the manœuvring on the other channels was the advantages of programmes being forty-five minutes long. So the new series of *Flog It!* was made to this length. That meant only one Insert instead of two, and fewer items going into auction. OK, the execs know best. However, starting a programme at a quarter to or past the hour seems less likely to capture the available audience than on-the-hour or half-hour starting times.

The next development threw the familiar patterns even further off course: Paul O'Grady jumped ship from ITV and took his pantomime act to Channel 4. ITV fought back with more celebrity vehicles: Richard Hammond's *5 O'Clock Show*, *The Sharon Osbourne Show*. Should *Flog It!* start earlier or later, the execs wondered. Would I do better against Sharon than Bob? Did *Flog It!* need to be different? Did I need to be different?

Mercifully it was decided simply to carry on, and monitor the daily audience ratings and channel share charts very carefully.

A few weeks later I saw one of the executives on Whiteladies Road, laughing and joking with a property programme production team. I caught his eye and asked him how the share was looking.

'Not so bad,' he explained. 'ITV have now stuck in *Grizzly Tales for Gruesome Kids*. You've seen off *SpongeBob SquarePants*.'

I felt relieved, proud even.

I'd held my end up, just by being me. They hadn't forced me to be different.

It would perhaps make a fitting epitaph for my gravestone: 'He saw off *SpongeBob SquarePants*.'

❖   ❖   ❖

This slightly bizarre episode set me thinking about the road that has taken me from music-obsessed teenager, to trend-setter, to antiques shop owner and then to presenter of BBC2's most popular daytime show.

I realised that I have had a chance to visit almost every part of the United Kingdom, with the special privilege on *Flog It!* of individual guided tours of many of the nation's most interesting buildings, museums, workshops, factories and artists' studios. I have been able to examine hundreds of wonderful artefacts and learn about their creation, use and heritage from their owners and some of Britain's foremost experts. Oh yes, and there's been the fun and fascination of meeting thousands of people who have happily given up a Sunday to bring a special possession along to a town hall to find out more about the object, learn of its potential value, and decide if they would like to see it go into auction, so that someone else can appreciate it in the future.

It's not possible to do justice to my thousands of visits to intriguing places in a single book, but over the last year I have tried to assemble and put into some sensible order my memories and experiences of more than twenty years of great British travel.

There are three intersecting journeys to be followed within the pages ahead. The first is chronological: a bit of biography and career path – in my case, paths, often somewhat crazed. Secondly I've attempted to reflect my immense appreciation for some wonderful buildings, artefacts and their makers. And thirdly I've tried to indicate the implications for a fellow in a small town shop who is suddenly catapulted from provincial obscurity, comfort and stability to inhabit a place in the corner of two million or more living rooms or kitchens for an hour almost every afternoon of the year.

Through *Flog It!* I've become, ironically, almost part of the furniture in people's homes; someone huge numbers of folk feel familiar with. I'm 'that bloke off *Flog It!*', for good or bad, and mostly it's the former, though there is a downside too, as you'll discover in the pages ahead. In essence this book is a celebration of our marvellous country, its landscapes, construction, contents and citizens. It's a colourful journey and you will collect, I trust, plenty of fresh perspectives and insights along the way. I hope I'll answer most of the questions I get asked whenever I turn up at a television location, or in a strange supermarket or café.

Whether you are a fan of the programme or not, welcome to my virtual coach trip for all ages (with some asides from the tour guide, who can release a few bees from his bonnet here that would definitely be out of place on television screens).

Come aboard for an enlightening and often amusing trip around Beautiful Britain, with dozens of stopping-off points where you can grab for yourself slices of fashion, samples of fine art and a selection of the extraordinary people, places, properties, problems and pleasures of *Flog It!*

Discussing shot choice with handheld cameraman Nathan Ridler.

2

Drum Beats

I took a fancy to drumming from an early age. When I was in the Cubs we occasionally formed a little military-style band, and I got the chance to wear and play a side-drum that I managed to master quite quickly. At about the same time I became aware that there was some serious inspiration living next door. This man occasionally asked my mum to look after his cat, because he was going to be away from home for a few nights. What did he do? Where did he go? Only on to stages to bang out top pop hits with his mates in front of a big, enthusiastic crowd. Wow. I was living in the same street as a successful rock drummer. From my West Molesey bedroom at the age of 8 I could occasionally hear Mick Avory wallop out a few phrases.

Paul Martin's Britain

From the front room I would witness him arriving by taxi at odd hours, looking stylish or scruffy but always exotic. And that's just how it should have been for the beat-man of the Kinks. This was in 1968, when they had just delivered 'Dedicated Follower of Fashion', Ray Davies's great song that supplied an ironic commentary on swinging London.

I wanted to be swinging. I wanted to be another Mick Avory. I persuaded Mum and Dad to buy me a second-hand drum kit and I stuck a picture of Mick on the side. The Kinks were in a super-league. With my school friends and neighbourhood mates we attempted to formulate bands and tunes. It was an ever-evolving activity. People would come and go, try and fail, argue over the agenda, see better prospects elsewhere, have conflicting goals. Some band wanabees saw the Beatles as their role models, others aimed at the territory occupied by the Rolling Stones, a few looked across the Atlantic and wished to capture something of the Beach Boys' beat. I was always trying to ape the Kinks.

I'm told that there are around a quarter of a million people in bands in Britain. I don't think there would have been so many back in the late sixties, but the power of pop and the search for breakthroughs in style, behaviour, sounds and status were immensely seductive. Undoubtedly I spent too much time trying to be an embryonic pop star, and not enough doing my homework or exam preparation, when suddenly I was wrenched away from this world of aspiration and promise.

My dad had got a new job – as head of the department of engineering and technology at Falmouth College. We were making a big move.

It was traumatic to leave London and arrive in the provinces, where people weren't as sharp, slick, knowing or smart, or so it seemed to me at the time. The West Country accents that I encountered added to the sense that I'd been cruelly dropped into the slow lane and would now have to move among unfashionable farming or fishing types with no appreciation of the trendy scene I had been torn away from.

I brought my drums down with me and my parents assured me I'd soon discover like-minded boys with an eye on finding the formula for the next hit and a look to go with it. Hadn't the Rolling Stones come from the provinces? People out in the sticks could appreciate and play music, and buy clothes that would look just fine on *Top of the Pops*.

But I was not convinced.

I had possibly been one tune away from emerging as part of the next sexy west London band; maybe on the very brink of musical fame. And instead I was stuck on some beach at the other end of the country. I spent a winter trudging across sand and sulking a lot.

Only in the spring did it dawn on me that this territory might actually have some appeal to the fashion-conscious. People came from London to enjoy the beaches. I lived right next to them. I could learn to surf like the locals. There was a trendy element to life in Falmouth after all, it had just taken me many months to realise it. So I became a beach bum, working up a fine tan, developing great confidence as a sea swimmer and getting a firm handle on surfing.

Notice I hadn't moved homework and studying up the agenda. Instead I had a new activity to pursue, for which you needed only a wet suit, a board and enough money to have a beer with the girls on the beach in the evenings.

I became a sort of hippy, and buddied up with Charlie Ardagh. Together we were cool dudes, adopting a poor man's flower-power look. At parties I would outrageously trade on my status: I'd been a close personal mate of Mick Avory of the Kinks. That cut quite a lot of ice, but Charlie had a claim to fame that Cornish boys found fascinating.

His aunt was Fiona Richmond. She was the glamorous, sexually unrepressed pin-up gracing the pages of *Men Only* that we sneaked

Family snaps: with Mum, Dad, my sister, Anne, and family pets.

a look at in the newsagent's. Across colourful spreads she revealed her gorgeous naked body. This was Charlie's aunt, and adding to her exotic reputation was the fact that her father was a local vicar, and yet on the high street anyone could view his offspring posing on a bed in her G-string, devoid of inhibition. These were heady thoughts for teenage boys.

Charlie seemed slightly embarrassed by the family connection. It was a two-headed monster. There was the prestige of his bloodline to those bronzed boobs in the top-shelf magazine, but he was also sullied by association. He aroused distaste in some households, where knowledge of his hereditary connections implied that he was a sexually deviant danger to the good and sensible folk of Falmouth. Well, I for one would never let Charlie feel isolated. He was my mate. And together we surfed, chatted up girls and listened to great music. We bought Rolling Stones, Jimi Hendrix and T-Rex albums and analysed every beat and bar, every word and phrase. To advance our appreciation of contemporary music, we decided to go where the scene was hot and the sounds were sharp: the summer rock festival in Great Windsor Park. This would place us where the action was, and chances were we'd meet up with some rock chicks who would be seriously impressed by a couple of beach boys with impeccable surfing credentials.

We thought long and hard about what to wear. The right look was imperative – ripped jeans and bell-sleeved T-shirts. We had to combine Cornwall cool with metropolitan mean. After several evenings anguishing over our inadequate wardrobes, we headed off with our rucksacks and tent to the A30 and stuck out our thumbs.

Our hitching efforts paid slow, steady dividends. Remember this was before the M5 and M4 came along, but we persevered and reached Slough by teatime on Friday. From there we invested in a bus to Windsor, where, in the temporary campsite, we set up our tent, checked out our appearance in a tiny shaving mirror, then headed into the throng and enjoyed a great evening watching a dozen good bands.

Around midnight it started to drizzle, then pour, but committed musical types like us would not be put off by such minor inconveniences. We hung on to the end, then, indifferent to a vicious downpour, wandered back to the campsite. It was dark, we were tired, we were drunk. We'd lost our bearings. We couldn't locate the right tent. There were thousands of them, and we had left ours without carefully registering any landmarks. We spent hours trudging up and down trying to identify Charlie's two-man tent without success. We were defeated by the rain and the dark, so spent the rest of the night under the flimsy awning of a Transit caravanette.

At dawn we recommenced our search and in military fashion worked logically across the square mile of temporary accommodation. After a couple of hours we concluded that our tent was not there. Someone had nicked it – along with everything inside. Now what?

For this photo opportunity, it was a good job that the tide was out. With Charlie and Jimmy, in my first school band.

We had a few pounds left. Just enough to catch a train from Windsor to Paddington, from where we walked to an address that might provide some tea and sympathy, the Whitehall Theatre. This was where Charlie's aunt worked. She played the lead in a farcical romp called *Pyjama Tops*, saucy stuff for its day. The photographs outside showed her in theatrical poses with her fellow thespians. Compromising positions within the proscerium arch.

We went round to the stage door and asked for Ms Richmond. The doorman told us to clear off. Charlie explained: 'She's my aunt.'

'Oh, yeah.' He told us to clear off more emphatically.

We reckoned that sooner or later she'd have to pass in or out of this door, so we hung around. Let's face it, we were now destitute. We sat on the pavement just a few hundred yards from Downing Street. Harold Wilson might have been at home, but did we care?

A woman came out of the stage door. Charlie leapt up and asked her when Fiona Richmond would be around. 'Not for hours.'

'She's my aunt,' explained Charlie. 'We had our tent and stuff stolen in Windsor.'

The woman decided that we were not a couple of trainee dirty old men lurking around for a glimpse of the sex queen, and so went back inside to phone Fiona.

Half an hour later a taxi arrived, and this tall, slim, blonde, tanned lady stepped out. This was Charlie's mother's younger sister. Charlie's mother was an average sort of mum. It was quite amazing to me that this stylish, supremely confident, alluring creature in a very short skirt could be a blood relative of the woman who was always telling me to take my dirty shoes off and not keep her son out so late in the evenings.

We did get tea and sympathy – in a café in Soho. Fiona had work commitments for her partner and employer, Paul Raymond. She occupied a small office up a couple of flights of stairs above Raymond's Revue Bar – London's number one, or possibly only, up-market stripclub. She told us we'd have to earn our keep. How? Appear on stage? Nope. Hand out flyers to passing tourists in Piccadilly Circus for the rest of the afternoon. Our reward was to go inside and see the show – providing we didn't tell our parents.

She made us tidy up a bit – the hippy look wasn't right for the Revue Bar. And so we sat with lots of dirty old men, a few with their wives or girl friends, watching a variety of girls strip, finally removing their G-strings before standing very still, which was the requirement of the legislation at the time. We were more bemused than aroused, but nevertheless it was a treat. We were treated to

Paul Martin's Britain

It was always good to have stylish photos on standby in case you got a call from the *New Musical Express*.

seeing Charlie's aunt strip off on the stage of the Whitehall, and Fiona took us to the apartment she shared with Paul, who was not around that weekend. She gave us a key and some money for supper, then left us there for the evening while she trod the boards and exposed that slick body to the masses. We had a spaghetti bolognese then returned to the flat and contemplated its style, status, luxury and lifestyle implications.

There was an address book by the gold-plated telephone. We couldn't resist examining the contents. There were famous names in there. I was struck by two magical words – Ringo Starr – next to a phone number. I was so tempted to make a note of this, but the sliver of logic still in my mind said I would never actually have a need for Ringo's phone number. There would never be an occasion when the right thing to do would be to ring Ringo and point out that, if he ever needed a night off from playing with the Beatles, I would be only too happy to step into the breach, and would not require a very big fee. No, that wasn't going to happen.

On Sunday morning Fiona took us by taxi to Paddington and paid for our tickets back to Falmouth. Two country boys now had a tale of exotic glamour to trade on at school and on the beach. The hippy who had stolen our tent had in effect done us a huge favour.

❖ ❖ ❖

Our Windsor and Whitehall weekend impacted on my thinking. It rekindled in me a sense of what I had lost when my family had moved away from the capital and how my drumming dreams had more chance of being fulfilled if I returned to the environment where lots of embryonic bands were casting around for new talent, fresh configurations, a catchy sound.

A couple of years later I finished college and returned to the big smoke. My goal? To make a breakthrough with a band. I'd got a few contacts and some old mates, and provided I was prepared to haul my kit about I could get some gigs. The money was poor but I was game to stick with it until the right chemistry got me into a bigger league. In the meantime, to help pay the bills, and utilise my Morris Traveller when the drum kit wasn't in the back, I started to work with a couple of pals putting stuff on Portobello Road market stalls. This venue, just north of Notting Hill, was starting to develop a reputation for trendiness. I looked a trendy sort of guy. Something about my appearance was vaguely reminiscent of David Essex, and this undoubtedly helped. I started to engineer my manner and appearance to give myself the aura of a young man who knows what's what in the swinging city.

With my mates I would undertake house clearances out in the leafy suburbs, spotting the bits and pieces that would make our stall the best place to buy accessories for the with-it home. The elements of my life now fell neatly into place. I looked good in a band and I looked good behind a stall on the Portobello Road. My car would house the drum kit a couple of evenings a week, and during the day transport furniture and furnishings from all around London to my flat, to be scrubbed up and laid out with flair on a Saturday morning.

This was paying my bills, and became my way of life for the next few years. I learned a heck of a lot about art history and fast sensed what was fashionable and saleable. It reached a point where I was determining what was fashionable. If it was on my

Just another average white band: still waiting for the big break iin my mid-twenties.

stall, it was, by definition, something worth having.

However, in my parallel nocturnal life I couldn't achieve the essential breakthrough. I loved drumming and was dedicated to becoming very good at it. The trouble is, drummers seldom lead bands. Phil Collins had done a great job with Genesis a few years earlier, but the core of any band lies on an arc, or often a short fuse, between the lead guitarist and the singer – if they are not the same person. Look at The Who – all hinges on Townsend driving Daltry.

The band is led from the front, hardly ever by the bloke with the drum kit, who takes up a lot of space and makes a lot of noise at the back, but is essentially a support of the front line and can seldom dominate it.

I was in dozens of bands that did good business. I was a reliable team player, never late, never troublesome, never losing the rhythm. But that wasn't enough to flourish. You needed a lucky break and that seemed to elude me.

Meanwhile, on Portobello Road things couldn't have been better. We were never short of customers. Not that this meant we became cavalier about what we would offer for sale. I think we really did have good judgement and a sense of the period, what worked and what wasn't right. We were trendy Londoners with our fingers on the pulse of fashion and worked hard at it.

And while I was usually eclipsed by the guitar-wielders when it came to impressing the girls at rock gigs, on the Portobello Road I was regularly chatted up. So I traded on this image that I had cultivated of being a man who knows what's what in fashion. Attractive young women would value my company and judgement. I had a great time.

One of the better bands I played in got a lot of good gigs performing pop standards for parties. A function band. We had a whole repertoire of numbers from what had been called the hit parade. This was jam on the bread and butter. No more sleeping in the van, without a change of clothing, living on café coffee and washing in café toilets.

We were invited to play for a birthday party for the actress Jane Seymour at a big house in Bath. It was an immensely glamorous occasion and we were the boys for the job. Instead of hanging around the car park waiting for our cue, we were invited to mingle with the guests, enjoy the buffet supper, sip the champagne. We relished this, and tried to behave as if this was our normal working environment. We were not a famous band, but on this evening we did our best to act like one.

We played our first set, which went down well, then it was back to that buffet. A very glamorous lady started talking to our lead singer. This was the way it was. He got the attention, which is how he always wanted it. But then it emerged that she wasn't an up-market groupie, but an entrepreneur. It was Elizabeth Emmanuel, a mover and shaker on the London scene. She was friendly with the guys in Sweet and matey with the boys in Mud. She knew people who might back us. We drove back to London that night full of excitement. Had the big break arrived?

Within two months we had made a record and shot a video to go with it – all dressed as cowboys, heading on horseback across Salisbury Plain. It was a horrible flop. Mercifully I had the day job to fall back on. But making that video had given me a couple of valuable contacts – people making films and doing photo shoots who were to be a vital element in my future life.

Good vibrations.

3

Finding a Style

I cultivated a shabby-chic style for myself and my stall. This worked immensely well, and the circles I moved in socially just added to my customer base and credibility. Thanks to some contacts, I started to get work providing the objects for photo shoots. An art director would indicate what he or she required and I would raid my store or set out for regional auction houses or antiques shops to track down suitable candidates.

The more I delivered the right objects and furnishings, the faster my reputation spread, and soon I was taking over from the art directors in deciding what would make a good setting for a fashion picture. I contributed to work that received exposure in all sorts of women's and lifestyle magazines. The images might grace a series of colour pages in *Marie Claire* or illustrate the fashion column of the London *Evening Standard*. Better outlets, better contacts, better life.

I had my first experience with the television industry at this time. A Sunday afternoon favourite was *The Clothes Show*, made at the BBC's Pebble Mill studios. The television industry had its own dedicated designers and setting experts and there was certainly no room for an outsider among the staffers who worked on the series. But a spin-off was in the offing, a stage show to be mounted at the new National Exhibition Centre on the outskirts of Birmingham. The television people had enough on their plates with the weekly Sunday show, and the construction and design of multiple stages and settings at this giant new exhibition space needed plenty of manpower, so I was given a role there on the basis of my work for the glossy magazines.

The event was planned for early December, but the build-up meant I was at work designing settings and acquiring props from early autumn. No one knew if the popularity of the television series would transfer to a huge shed, but young women turned up in their thousands to see the models, designs and television presenters in the flesh.

I was very self-conscious about my efforts. For a photo shoot, everything has to look perfect but only momentarily and only from one angle. At the NEC we were dealing with multi-dimensions, and so every catwalk had to work from every line of sight, both for the audience and for the cameras. This event became a key milestone in my calendar of commitments. I had to leave the Portobello Road responsibilities to my mates from September to Christmas each year.

Another bonus of the NEC event was that, on the final day for the final few hours, you could buy lots of great clobber at bargain prices. Anything on a hanger could be had for a few pounds. There was no desire to take the stock back to the fashion houses it had come from. So I did an annual shop for my own clothes, spending very little, but getting some high-fashion stuff for my wardrobe.

I still did the odd drumming gig. I was in a group that supported the Average White Band for a while, and this made me think we would never be anything other than an average white band. I enjoyed playing, and preferred performing jazz to running through standards or blundering around with numbers the singer had made up believing it had the potential to be a future Number One.

This was my life in my late twenties. Being part of the fashion scene and acting as a conduit for stylish period artefacts for people's homes meant I moved in elevated circles. Not that I had to go far for that. Charlotte Rampling lived across the road, the woman who wrote Mary Poppins was just down the street, Maggie Thatcher's home on Flood Street backed on to mine and I frequently bumped into Bob Geldof, who was always busy doing

When searching for a style, go back to your roots; to understand wood in its cut and felled form, you have to appreciate it in its living organic setting.

something in the neighbourhood, though I never found out what. My most vivid memory is of making a fool of myself in front of someone I hugely revered.

Olivia Harrison, wife of George, was a great client. I was invited to her house in Maidenhead to talk through a project. I wondered if I would meet George, but he was away in the States, playing with the Travelling Willoughbys. I clicked with Olivia and was invited to undertake more assignments under her wing. A few months later I again had reason to go over to Maidenhead. I was thinking solely of the task in hand when into the living room walked George Harrison with Roy Orbison.

Now believe it or not I could take George in my stride. After all, wasn't he just one of the many provincial boys who had messed about in bands for many years, like me? Yes, he'd got good breaks, and was immensely talented, but I thought of myself as essentially out of the same stable. Whereas Roy was a god. And I treated him like one, by which I mean I was a bumbling, stumbling, muttering, sweating, complete imbecile in his presence. He was charming and gracious and must have thought I was mentally retarded.

I seldom had time to get down to Cornwall to see my parents, then I got a call from Mum to say that Dad was not well. He was diagnosed with cancer and deteriorated very quickly. I travelled back and forth from London to Falmouth and watched him decline with horror.

At least the M4 and M5 were open now so I could make the journey more quickly, and on the way would pop into antiques centres so I could make use of the time spent travelling.

My father passed away, which devastated my mother and me.

I had a sense of time passing and a feeling that the chaos of my life in London was not in my long-term interests. Should I move away from the big city and go and support my mum at the other end of the country? I'd often stopped somewhere around the

Savernake Forest in Wiltshire on my journeys between homes. I quite abruptly decided to escape to that tree-dense paradise. No phone calls, no deadlines to meet, no fashion target to reach. But I took my drum kits. I calmed myself down by living in a simple cottage with my collection of artefacts housed in a nearby barn.

I was in limbo, waiting to find a new style.

Me and my mum.

23

4

In Praise of Brown Leaves

I'm an autumn animal. That's my season. It's when good things happen to me, and when I feel most at one with the world. The colours of the leaves bring out the best in me. The cool air replaces the summer heat and I see the array of changes as the greenery starts to fade and decline, and the oranges, yellows and browns start to emerge across the branches. It's not a time of dying, it's a time of tranquillity. Those leaves have done their job, delivering energy and fuel to the fruit.

I am at one with the evolving colours of nature at this time, immensely appreciative of their charm and power. That slice of the spectrum from green to red enriches my heart and soul, and gives me strength and an inner peace. I think people subconsciously recognise this. They like me across these months, and I like them.

Paul Martin's Britain

That doesn't mean I'm a crabby fellow the rest of the year, just that my sense of aliveness, of purpose and fulfilment, is strongest from September to November. Those months give me so much, and I like to think that I return the favours.

When I was involved in art direction, I often found myself working with people who were slaves to colour charts. They carried with them every available sample of shade options, and would anguish over which tone to go for. Frankly I felt some of them were colour-blind, or perhaps their clients were. I was never burdened by all that anxiety over the vast choice.

I am firmly of the belief that mother nature has the answers, achieved through evolution, and that our eyes are in harmony with her work. If you want to know what colours will go together, simply examine what the natural world has juxtaposed. See the colour of a strawberry, then look at the colour of the leaf

In Praise of Brown Leaves

alongside. They work together in the fruit field. And they will work together in your home.

I am especially drawn to the colours of autumn, the rustic reds, the russet browns. Pick up a bruised apple and you will find a rich array of chromatic hues. Here's your home decorating palette. Track down the paint or other materials that capture these characteristics and you won't go far wrong. The best plan is to combine the artificial paint with some natural materials. So good, honest wood will always enhance a space, bringing natural dignity to an artificial setting.

This puts me a long way from the world of the Scandinavian sheds full of metal and glass, mixed with sheets of plastic mockingly presented as timber. Chipboard was a great invention for mass producing utilitarian objects for open-plan offices, but I don't like it in living spaces. It is essentially disharmonious, and I

Paul Martin's Britain

am sure people would have happier lives if they were more at one with nature in their living rooms. In my kitchen I have a simple wicker gate acting as a utensil rack. I found the sweet, unique object at an antiques fair. I cleaned it up and hung a few meat hooks on it. Now it holds my saucepans and looks timeless. It is not the product of an instant furniture factory. It has a history, a sense of being manipulated by a craftsman who has left a heritage.

We can daily treasure his work and eye. No off-the-shelf shelf can match that legacy, that contribution to the richness of our world.

I relished my time in Savernake forest, living in a simple cottage in a very simple manner. The house had been owned by an elderly couple who had established a very serviceable vegetable

In Praise of Brown Leaves

Being creative with function and form.

garden, and this went on to serve me extremely well. I had taken a dramatic leap from the Kings Road, Chelsea to a dense, minimally managed woodland. I had been existing in a maelstrom of sensual London stimuli – shops, restaurants, people, clothes, activities, noise. Now I was alone with the trees. But every one of these fine monuments to mother nature spoke to me, communicated with me about how the world works, how time passes, and how little impact any human being has upon the bigger picture of life on earth.

This wasn't a culture shock for me after London. I came to realise that I had been suffering from shock after so long sucking in the electricity of the city. Now I was calming down, allowing nature to determine my options, my speed, my parameters.

5

Position in the Provinces

ach morning in Savernake I awoke to the sounds of birds in the trees, as opposed to the non-stop traffic of the King's Road. I looked out of my window at trees, not terraces of houses changing hands for more than a million pounds.

I was the big disturbance round here, because I belted seven bells out of my drums. There was no one to annoy. Perhaps I agitated the birds, but I like to think the trees appreciated the company and the tremors through their trunks that my serious hammering would have caused. I wasn't completely at one with nature. I would have had to abandon my £5,000 worth of drums to do that. But I was getting the swinging city out of my head and my heart.

Paul Martin's Britain

It had been great to be part of that scene, but now I was recognising what I had slowly started to appreciate when the family moved to Falmouth: the natural elements in our beautiful world. In Cornwall the sea and coastline made the biggest impact. In the heart of Wiltshire it was the fields, the greenery, the skies that enchanted my eye, soothed my soul. And I came to wonder how I had sustained all the self-imposed pressure I had endured every waking hour in the city.

Dwelling on my father's swift demise made me question what I wanted out of life in the longer term. We are on this earth for a finite time. I felt that as he approached his death he had a sense of satisfaction at his achievements. If I had been a disappointment, he never showed it. I made it clear to him that I would look after Mum, and this I had started to do by moving halfway from London so I could reach her in a couple of hours, spending most weekends with her. And that's what I did for quite some time.

I needed to earn a living. At Savernake I could return to London easily, but my appetite for the weekend shenanigans on the Portobello Road had dramatically declined. I couldn't be the guy with his finger on the fashion pulse if I was spending the week in an artisan's frugal dwelling in the middle of a forest. No, I needed new territory to occupy. One of the first occupations I undertook from my new home was to give drumming lessons. OK, I wasn't Mick Avory or Ringo Starr, but I had years of professional experience under my belt, and there are always teenagers eager to acquire the skills that might take them up the steep slopes of pop mountain. I tutored half a dozen youngsters, and then was asked to run evening classes at Swindon Technical College, and some sessions at Marlborough College.

I was using some part of my acquired experience and handing it on to others, and that has always given me pleasure. It does not require financial reward. It is one of the aspects of *Flog It!* that I

most appreciate – sharing my knowledge with others, to enrich their
appreciation. My giving to them in
effect gives to me.

At 28, freshly arrived in
Marlborough.

Helping youngsters with dreams in
their head to handle the drums caused
me to dwell further on my preoccupa-
tions of the previous decade, chiefly
believing every band was the next
potential vehicle for the big breakthrough – if only this, if only that. If
only a hip producer or A and R man
had been in the bar that night when we were brilliant. It was
amazing to us how we could never recreate that magical night,
and how the next time we played in a pub we seemed so ordinary
again.

I'd done a few trips from Harwich to Rotterdam – in the best
traditions of early Beatles adventures. I felt terrible on those North
Sea crossings and struggled with some awful down-market Dutch
catering. On one occasion I was distinctly unwell when it was
time for us to go on stage. Moments before our set began I threw
up – across my drum kit. The lights were down so no one else
saw the mess I was literally in, but there was no time for me to
nip to the loo and clean up. We were on, so I had to play for an
hour with a dreadful mess and growing smell emerging from my
jeans and shoes. The rest of the band steadily became aware of
the disgusting situation I was in. Afterwards they ribbed me
endlessly, and my arguments about my determined professionalism just cut no ice.

The kids I was teaching in Wiltshire all had their heroes, as I
had had mine. They talked of who they wanted to emulate, and I
recalled having said something similar about Charlie Watts or
Nick Mason when I was their age. I'd been a good jobbing

Avebury, the oldest stone circle in the world, and an opportunity to escape for inspiration.

musician; at 30, however, you realise you have probably reached your ceiling. And, of course, as the most successful rock icons always remind us, you never have total control in a band. You are dependent on your colleagues to succeed. Like a marriage, it can't carry on without the commitment of each partner. And frequently this interdependence and necessary subjugation can be very painful. With antiques you have control over your destiny. In a band you will ever remain dependent on others.

I nipped into Marlborough for a bit of shopping every now and again. Its high street has timeless dignity – fine buildings only occasionally marred by chain store frontages and modern structures. Devizes pleased me, too, and I liked the busyness and purpose of Swindon, where I could get a brief reminder of big city bustle, albeit without the moneyed poseurs of the King's Road.

I knew masses about antique furniture. I had visited most of the auction houses in this part of the world, and had been inside most of the antique shops in the region at some time or other, particularly if I was looking to satisfy the wishes of a particular London client for whom money was no object.

I reckoned there could be something of a gap in the local antiques trade: a shop specialising in period oak and quality mahogany. Could I be the man to fill it? Should I, could I, establish a retail business around here? Marlborough seemed the right size, with a promising customer base – the county set who shopped at Waitrose, the parents of the children at the private schools. These people had the money and potentially the appreciation of what I could offer. Who knows, they might have been the very same folk who had perambulated down the Portobello Road ten years previously and had now settled out here in the up-market sticks.

There will always be lots of adequate drummers around, but someone with a sense of style, a feeling for art and an instinct for retail theatre is less common.

In London I was a small fish in a big lake. Here I could possibly be a big fish in a modest pond. I had always liked the notion of the self-made millionaires who started their businesses with a pile of goods in a hand cart. I decided to give it a go, and started looking for premises.

6

In the Right Place at the Right Time

For once I was in the right place at the right time. There I was in a barn with a load of antiques, but I didn't get a lot of passing trade. So one day I was doing my shopping in Marlborough when I saw an empty shop with accommodation above, and I thought this would be an ideal place to deal in antiques. I could get rid of my house and the barn, and sell my antiques from this beautiful Regency building in the widest high street in Britain.

So for three years I wore seven hats: I was the buyer, the seller, the restorer, the delivery man, the accountant, the PR man and the cleaner. And I worked hard. The first year I was funding the business, the second I broke even, and the third year it started to look after me and I was able to employ some part-time staff.

Finally, in the right place at the right time.

Then one day I was sitting in my shop with my feet up on the desk reading the *Antiques Trade Gazette*, planning my next buying tour in Wales, when a lady with a camera walked in saying she was a researcher with the BBC in Bristol, working on a new antiques programme. This was Patsy Titcombe, who has affectionately become Aunty Titcombe, the woman who discovered me. We got talking and I discovered she had started out life as 'Patsy's Prizes' wearing pink dungarees handing out the prizes on Noel Edmonds's *Swap Shop*. She was still wearing dungarees, but thankfully not pink!

Patsy got me talking to camera about some of the furniture in the shop, extolling their virtues and social history. It was all too easy to try and sell her something; she was the only person who had walked into the shop that day. But two hours later I realised she wasn't interested in the furniture: she was interested in me. She decided to send the recording off to the daytime controller Jane Lush. Two days later I had a phone call from her PA, asking me to forward a CV. I cobbled one together and walked over the road to the dress shop and asked them to send a fax for me to BBC London. Ten minutes later I had a phone call back saying that they thought I had the potential to be a TV presenter. How would I like a screen test?

Initially I said no. I had spent three years starting up a business, and I couldn't turn my back on it. I was loving it so much, it was oxygen for me. I talked it over with a few friends in the wine bar that night. They all fell about laughing, saying I was going to be the new Dale Winton doing *Supermarket Sweep*. So I rang the BBC and declined. But they replied, 'Well there is a catch. This is a programme about antiques. We want you to be the new face of antiques, and it can only be good for your business.'

So, I thought, why not?

Primitive Welsh cupboard settle, c. 1750. A fitted kitchen for a small Welsh cottage, known as a cupboard settle. The box lid would lift to reveal a storage compartment for salt, potatoes, fuel, etc. In the panelled back, the three doors would open to reveal a fitted interior, storage for spices, preserves, cheese, bread, fruit and other supplies. Notice the locks; spices were valuable, so were under lock and key.

A primitive oak Welsh chair, c. 1720–40. Because of its very naive form, it becomes functional sculpture. It is a work of art. Try and find me another!

7

New Boy in the Class

I have strong recollections of Rotherham, because this was where I first purposefully stuck my face in front of a television camera and tried to adopt the manner and style of someone who knows something worth knowing, with a capacity to put that knowledge across. That was more than six years ago, and when I look back on my early efforts, I cringe. I was so naive and clunky.

I suppose most people who become television presenters have had a previous life that somehow prepared them for the cameras. They may have been newspaper journalists, or radio reporters, or college lecturers or media graduates. Yes, they'd been doing something that developed ability to gather information and express it appropriately, while talking into a dark ring of glass as if

Paul Martin's Britain

Location: Arkwright's water mill in Matlock, Derbyshire; interviewing a local historian.

A standalone piece-to-camera, top and tailing the show.

they were standing in the corner of someone's living room or kitchen. Nothing in my previous life had quite prepared me for this weird behaviour.

I was used to nattering to people in the antiques trade and to customers, but suddenly I was required to speak to a strange person who is at home in the afternoon and who doesn't know me. And that person doesn't know very much about antiques, and frankly doesn't care that much either, and might at any second decide they would rather watch Carol Vorderman cheerfully solving number puzzles on the adjacent channel.

I had to learn how to function effectively in these peculiar circumstances.

It wasn't easy.

My first task was to turn up at the Wilkinson and Bayton auction house. The valuation day had already taken place at the Royal Crown Derby factory shop, and I was going to provide the seamless links that would structure the whole programme. I'd been given a collection of scripts to read and learn a few days earlier. On the floor of the auction room, in front of a bunch of strangers, I was now supposed to look into the lens of an enormous, menacing camera and speak the words in the script.

Rather than let the tension build up, I decided to have a go straightaway. As soon as the camera and I were positioned where the director requested, I started to speak the words, and by some miracle got through to the end of the first script without a flaw (and without breathing). This wasn't going to be so bad then.

The director seemed quite pleased, but the cameraman wasn't so sure. Well, it was a start, wasn't it?

No. I hadn't had a microphone on me.

What?

I'd assumed the big furry thing on the front of the camera was hearing my voice.

Apparently not. I had to have a radio microphone stuffed down my shirt. The microphone itself is the black bit that sometimes clips on to the edge of my collar and is sometimes hidden under my jacket. A wire runs from this to the top of my trousers, where a little black box transmits my voice digitally to a matching black box carried by the sound recordist, who normally lurks around directly behind the cameraman, to whom he is attached by more cables.

The sound recordist carries a portable audio mixing console, slung around his shoulders on straps. He wears headphones to evaluate the sound and sends a satisfactory electronic version of this to the camera itself, so it can be recorded alongside the pictures on the tape in the cassette. (I could go into media studies lecturing on the strength of this!)

The point is, I'd made an admirable stab at delivering the first bit of dialogue (or piece-to-camera, as we say in the trade), but unfortunately I'd done it all too soon. The camera wasn't recording, and the microphone wasn't connected.

Apart from that, I'd made a promising start.

First big lesson: don't bother opening your mouth until others say they are ready to look at you and listen to you. The camera is recording only when the camera person says so. You can't even rely on the little red light on the front, because sometimes the cassette tape has not come up to speed, and you have to wait for the person looking in the viewfinder to let you know when this is the case. Equally, don't bother uttering your dialogue until the sound recordist or director has told you to do so. It's wrong to assume that, even if you have a microphone stuck on your shirt the operator has turned up the volume and is feeding your sounds to the camera's recording head.

Needless to say, once I had grasped the elements of this system, I was completely unable to replicate what had worked so well before they were ready for me. It was painful – for all parties. I couldn't get the words right again, and I was witnessing out of the corner of my eye a trio of professionals sinking in spirits as they became convinced they'd got the wrong man for the job.

The director decided to move on to another script. He'd come back to the first one later.

I was moved to another position and told to deliver script number two, but not until the director called 'Action!'. Now, you've heard that word, haven't you? It's how they make films.

Everything for a scene is prepared, then a man in a baseball cap sitting on a folding chair yells that triggering expression and suddenly stuff happens in front of the camera. At the end of this he-who-must-be-obeyed shouts 'Cut!', and everything stops.

OK, that's the world of Hollywood movies, but I never expected the same principles to be applied here, where little old me just had to do a few little old links. But they did expect this, and it freaked me out.

'Action!' Suddenly I couldn't remember who I was, where I was or what I was supposed to be doing here, never mind what I should be saying. That terminology was scary. It was for professionals, and I wasn't one. The cheery director assured me I'd get the hang of it, but I feared inside that he was wasting his time and I was wasting mine.

I tried again.

'Action!' The term froze me. It stimulated inaction.

'Once more, please.' The director assured me it would go well now.

'Action!' I'd forgotten how to open my mouth. Had I picked up lockjaw from someone in the crowd?

'What's the problem?' the hovering producer now enquired.

'I think it's that word,' I mumbled in embarrassment.

'What word?' he wondered, looking at his dog-eared copy of the script. Had they put in there a term I wasn't familiar with? Was I dyslexic and had kept quiet about it?

'Action,' I said.

'That's my line,' came the witty reply.

'No, I mean that's what's throwing me. That word. I . . .'

'What about "Go!"?'

'That would be better.'

Go! I know. I had run in school sports days on the strength of Go! Well, Go! with Three-Two-One in front.

'OK. Stand by. Recording. Go!'

I was still empty-headed and silent.

'Go!'

Nothing.

'Gooooooo!'

I could recall the whole of my past life, but not the first words of the script I was now supposed to be speaking at that nasty, intruding, insensitive ring of glass.

'What about Three-Two-One?'

'What about it?' snapped back the director.

'In front of the Go!, please,' I whinged.

If ever you wanted to witness a theatrical raising of the eyebrows and accompanying sharp intake of breath, this was the moment.

He did it as if he was on the stage of the Palladium, determined to grip the attention of the back row of the upper circle. And it was all for my benefit, merely 5 feet away.

'Recording. Stand by. Three-Two-One, Go!'

'Hello and welcome to *Flog It!*, the antiques show where the bric-à-brac in your attic could earn you a small fortune at auction.'

This was it. I'd broken my duck.

The team cheered up.

'Very good. Let's just try another.'

I agreed, and managed a second delivery.

They liked this.

I wasn't so sure, and thought I could do it better.

OK, another take.

And this one seemed to flow better still. I had regained a sense of confidence. Felt vaguely like a human being once more.

Three-Two-One. I was up and running.

All I had to do now was ask some questions of auctioneer Paul Bayton about the *Flog It!* lots, then turn up the next day and stand between the participants and our experts, James Braxton

and Nigel Smith, as each of the items went under the hammer. The following day I undertook my first two Insert film recordings. One was aboard the Darley Dale Railway train, where I talked to Jackie and Jeremy while stuffing my mouth full of Bakewell pudding, after which I got a ride on the locomotive footplate. Mmm, this television business wasn't so bad. Then on to the Crown Derby factory, where I watched talented staff turn out plates, before having a go myself and failing miserably to plonk a circular slice of clay on to the centre of a revolving base.

But what did I care. I was up and running. Somehow or other I'd got myself on the telly.

Making the most of the natural light.

8

Turning a Profit

When I started doing *Flog It!*, I had to learn many new skills, but one thing that required no new comprehension on my part was spending time in auction houses, because I had been doing that for years. I had bought and sold furniture and furnishings for more than a decade in auctions, on market stalls and in shops. I had a pretty good idea of what would turn a profit and where. And, despite having to take on a whole raft of new responsibilities as a television presenter, in the early days I found it impossible not to want to carry on buying things that I could perhaps later sell in my shop in Marlborough.

In fact I imagined the television work would allow me to visit auction houses that would normally be off my radar, and so find promising pieces to take back to Wiltshire to do up and display on my premises. I hadn't realised that the new job would be so demanding in terms of time and concentration, or that I would have little energy or appetite to be trading in oak between assignments and screen appearances.

If you saw those early shows, as well as witnessing my clumsy attempts to cut the mustard as a television presenter, you also saw an antiques dealer doing television links between trying to turn a profit for his business. On the auction days, when not working up to announce one of the valuation items, I might bid for other things in the sale, then face the problem of how to take them away when I was due to record an Insert the next day or head to Bristol for voice-over sessions.

I travelled round in my beaten-up Volvo – the standard issue vehicle for furniture dealers. And I would frequently take Bluebell, my beloved German Shepherd, with me, because that's what I'd done before the television work came along.

I was addicted to being an antiques dealer, always looking for the bargain that could become a profitable sale. To buy something for £200 and sell it for £400 is a simple but effective pleasure. You need to factor in transport costs, overheads and tax. It's impossible to cost in your time realistically, but against that you have the pleasure of studying and, albeit briefly, owning a beautiful object, then giving someone else the pleasure of having it in their possession. The good thing with a shop is that you can develop a customer base: people who know you and like your eye and style. You may not be currently stocking anything they want, but if your general style has appealed to them, there's a good chance they will come back for another look.

Quite often someone will tell you what they are looking for, and this then gives you a remit to try to track down a satisfactory article. I would often take mobile phone numbers, and if I came across a table or cabinet that seemed right for that client, would ring them to describe what I'd found, and ask if they thought I

should buy it with them in mind. You can't guarantee the client will take the item from you, so you have to achieve a price that will allow you to sell it on somewhere and not be totally reliant on a phone description and half-promise for your sale.

The greatest reward is that look of pleasure on people's faces when they see what they really want. That always made me feel good. The fact they then wrote a cheque in my favour was an excellent bonus, of course.

Poor old Bluebell. She has been in more auction rooms and hotel rooms than any other mutt in the country.

Paul Martin's Britain

As the success of *Flog It!* grew and the schedulers wanted more editions of the programme, the practicality of combining my business with television presenting declined. I had to concentrate on one or the other, and I eventually decided to go with the television work, knowing I could always return to antiques full-time when the British public, or a new programme controller, decided they had had enough of me. So I eventually closed the shop down, and later moved out of my flat above it. It's now a dress shop on Kingsbury Street. Number 4 if you're interested.

But the bug of buying hasn't gone away. And while now I know I don't have to service my retail business, I am still drawn to finding something I really like that seems underpriced for some reason. I still bid for things in auction, simply with a view to owning them and enjoying them. Everyone in the field dreams of buying something for £25 and selling it for a couple of thousand. Such unlikely but magical prospects keep many a modest trader focused on the task, even though it so seldom happens. I know of one furniture dealer in Somerset who acquired a whole collection of items from a house clearance, and hadn't had a chance to evaluate them carefully. A man then wandered into the big tin shed and noticed a grubby old chair among the newly arrived stock. He offered the dealer a hundred pounds for it. The dealer took his cheque, considering he had now turned a profit on his house-clearance activities. Later he was told the chair was an early Chippendale worth around £9,000.

The lesson here is that you're always learning, and you never know it all. Study, evaluate, ask questions, compare notes. Make measured decisions when planning to buy, and maximise the appeal when about to sell.

In the second series of *Flog It!* we undertook a valuation day at The Lawn in Lincoln, with David Barbie and Michael Bagott doing the honours. These two guys demonstrate they know their stuff time and time again, and for a novel Insert film they decided to put me to the test. I was to go to a huge antiques centre not far from Lincoln and find something that I could sell at a Grantham auction house and make a profit on. I was allowed one and a half hours on the premises to choose a piece. This proved a monumental challenge. The antiques centre claims to be the largest in Europe. Well, it certainly consists of many rooms on many floors and was certainly the biggest I'd ever discovered. I toyed with the idea of a painting but didn't spot anything priced sufficiently competitively. There was plenty of furniture, but I couldn't be sure anything would sell well at Grantham. A good guide is to look for something that is clearly an antique, is well made, decorative and also functional.

With merely a few minutes to go – and no, this wasn't a contrivance for the camera, I genuinely almost ran out of time – I spotted a dusty old bundle of carefully shaped sticks joined with some brass hinges. What was it? I picked it up and gingerly opened an artist's easel. I got it for £15 and polished it up, then put it into the Golding and Young sale. And I was very pleased that it fetched £40, which, after the seller's commission, left me with a profit of £21.25. I could hold my head up high in the presence of David and Michael – who then did the decent thing and bought me a drink.

The business of antiques is a fascinating combination of an appreciation of beauty, a thirst for knowledge and the pursuit of precious objects or wealth. It's driven by human greed and can be as addictive as gambling. However much someone appreciates the art in the item, the monetary worth is always in the back of their mind, and seeing the value increase is a delicious feeling.

9

How Flog It! *Works*

You are at home on a typical weekday afternoon, and, at some time between 3 and 6 p.m., Yours Truly turns up on BBC2, welcoming you to a town or city, introducing a couple of antiques experts, who, in a suitably large, dry space, talk through items of interest with four owners. After that I miraculously appear at an auction house a couple of weeks after the valuation event and discuss with the auctioneer the prospects for some of these items.

Now I am joined by the owner and together with the expert who assessed the item we watch the auctioneer seek bids for the item. Fingers crossed it reaches the recommended reserve, then passes that point to rise through the price range the expert has estimated and eventually go beyond that to a finishing point pleasantly above all original expectations.

Leicester market on Sunday morning looking for a good spot for a piece-to-camera. The crew is obviously hoping to get some footage for an out-take.

Next I appear in a museum, workshop, studio or shop to explore a topic related to collecting or a historical archive.

Then we're back in the town hall or sports hall with four more items to be assessed for their owners. After that I'm in another interesting place associated with antiques, art history or heritage. Now we're back in that auction house and the final four participants witness the progress of their items in the sale.

That's what you get on telly. How is it done in practice?

Preparation, preparation, preparation, preparation. Is that enough preparations?

The *Flog It!* production office is in the BBC centre in Bristol, a very fine building on Whiteladies Road with an Egyptian look to its modern architecture. The major functions on the site are the Natural History Unit – editing all the wonderful stable of programmes presented by David Attenborough and his protégés – *Antiques Roadshow*, BBC regional television and local radio, and then the returning series and one-off production departments.

I suppose *Antiques Roadshow* is the longest-running regular element of the BBC1 schedule. You can't really imagine a winter on television without the Sunday teatime treat. But we must never assume that the landscape is immune to earthquakes. Who would have imagined that *Tomorrow's World*, *Grandstand* and *Top of the Pops* could disappear? Unlike many fields of manufacturing where the customer requires the same product again and again, television is generally an evolving proposition, with the controllers and planners constantly tweaking the mix, taking what is available and deploying it most appealingly, commissioning something new in the hope it finds an audience and draws people away from other options. So producers, directors, researchers and production coordinators are deployed in different ways at different times to initiate and deliver a new television formula.

No one knew if the *Flog It!* formula would last. Somehow, mercifully, it has now reached its sixth year, and with so many episodes being made each season, the production requirements are among the most demanding at Whiteladies Road. The team have to find valuation venues, available antiques experts and auction houses happy to have a disruptive and noisy bunch of strangers milling about in their midst. In parallel, researchers are scouting for stately homes, museums, centres of excellence, studios, workshops or collectors' dens where I can turn up and explore a topic that will result in a five-minute Insert film.

All of which, as you can imagine, represents quite a portfolio of preparation.

Each valuation day and auction sale will deliver three pro-grammes. For example, we visit Leeds Corn Exchange one Sunday but record not just eight, not just sixteen, but twenty-four people talking about the heirloom they no longer want on their mantelpiece. So we have the spine for three separate shows from that considerable investment in a crew taking over the premises for the day and drawing in 700 people with bagfuls of posses-sions. A team of directors, cameramen, sound recordists, researchers and runners are deployed to cover the work. There's more than one of everyone – apart from little old me.

That's the only way it can work. It's efficient mass production in order to make me look cool and casual as I wander effortlessly between experts and cheery local people waiting in queues to see if they have something exciting. If you've been to a valuation day, you will know that there are three cameras recording something or other almost non-stop and several directors organising foreground and background, all so that I can drift with balletic ease between parts of the room.

Paul Martin's Britain

It's 9.30. The doors are just about to open. The crowd's here. So let's get the show on the road.

A town hall. A typical valuation day. What patience and enthusiasm, sometimes to hear your family treasure is worth absolutely nothing!

The trick is that I look into the right ring of black glass and talk to you at home and let the director, cameraman and sound recordist make sure it's all correctly framed and cleanly captured. There is also a team of off-screen experts providing assessments to the constantly moving queue of visitors. The on-screen experts consult the off-screen gang to identify and evaluate potential on-camera prospects, as well as browsing through the queues before they reach the interior setting. Runners are allocated to manage the queue, organising the people moving along the rows of seats so that everyone reaches a valuation table in turn in a fair and unfussy way. The chosen few who are asked to sit in front of the cameras then have to be quizzed over their availability for the subsequent auction. If they agree to the whole process, we take their objects from them and wrap them up safely for transportation to the auction venue.

So, at the end of that day, we have the tapes to make up part of three programmes. At some point over the next few days – to minimise travel and overnight accommodation – a couple of

directors, a camera crew, a researcher and I will move on to the chosen museums and collections. For the three programmes we require three six Insert films, so we devote a half a day to each subject. Half a day to film within Highclere Castle or Avebury, the Royal Worcester porcelain factory or Souter Lighthouse. This requires swift, effective decision-making by the directors, and no messing by the crews or me. It's an immensely taxing undertaking, with no fall-back position.

For reasons of economy and efficiency, two Insert films are recorded each day. And everyone needs a lunch break – at lunch time, not in the middle of the afternoon. Exteriors need light, and in winter that means outside shots must be 'in the can' by 3.30 p.m., otherwise it looks weirdly dark. So we brutally move through the morning, shooting pieces-to-camera from me, interviews with experts or curators, and illustrative footage showing detail and settings. The aim is to have all that is needed by 12.30 p.m. so that everyone can take a lunch break and then drive to the next location for 2 p.m., for another intensive four hours of filming to give us the second Insert of the day. Next day, same system – one film in the morning, another in the afternoon. Same crew, same me, but often a different director, because the concentration level is too extreme for the same person to make all the necessary decisions on picture and narrative on consecutive days. Directors need some thinking and preparation time in advance and some recovery time immediately afterwards – in an ideal world.

So now we have our valuation material and our Insert footage. All we need now is a pair of visits to the auction house. Why a pair of visits? First we turn up on the preview day and pick some items to talk about with the auctioneer. This might take a couple of hours of his time and ours, but it has to be done in advance of the auction, because none of us has time on the auction day itself. Remember you see eight auction items in the programme, but twenty-four lots from *Flog It!* face the cameras on that auction day.

So three camera crews gather to shoot me, the auctioneer, the experts and our guests, plus punters bidding for lots from the floor. Our researchers and runners prepare detailed notes on each object and its owner; we have already negotiated for each of our lots to be auctioned at a tolerable rate through the day to allow for change-over – moving the right member of the public and *Flog It!* expert into position, each with a microphone tucked into their clothes, so you see a smooth, casual grouping having fun observing one fascinating sale.

Yes, there is frenetic work going on behind the scenes to deliver these moments of cheery conversation from a corner of the room. Imagine the nuisance factor we create with our manipulation of lights, cameras and people every few minutes, while others are trying to earn a living or acquire a precious object right alongside us.

May I please take this opportunity to convey my appreciation, on behalf of the BBC and all *Flog It!* fans, for the tolerance, patience, kindness and decency that we enjoy at the auctions? Thank you for having us, and for putting up with us. Thank you, thank you and thank you again.

We have now got the constituent parts of three programmes in the can. Someone takes all these back to Bristol, where a team of editors starts to shape the footage into meaningful, pleasing forms. And that's just from one valuation venue. The very next week, often the very next day, some of us are out on the road doing it all again.

We have a stable of experts, a stable of camera crews and back-up staff, but we have just one me. So another whole *Flog It!* machine must descend on another town or city and power through the same sequence of processes once again, always cheerful, always looking for the best subject for the camera, always with an eye to good health and safety practice, always with a sense of being neat and efficient and using our budget in the most sensible way. We have been making eighty programmes in a year recently, which keeps us pretty busy.

OK, television anoraks, can you take any more? We have just reached post-production. The tapes shot on location have arrived in the editing suites. Here the editors and directors have a few days to skim through the footage, built a narrative order for each programme and start to illustrate the detail of the objects and places covered. They will also write some script to fill the bits between the interviews and my pieces-to-camera. Now the producer calls in and has a first viewing of each programme. He'll be looking for sense and performance and order. Are we saying the right things in the right way? Do people on screen look good and sound good? Can we see all we need to see to be able to understand what each object is and where we are? Have we got the best order for the valuation items? Bear in mind that, if there are eight items, then the permutations of order in the finished programme run into hundreds. And in what order should the Insert films appear? There are three to be deployed across three programmes. We have already tried to allocate an appropriate order, but sometimes the dialogue at the venue or the auction house will conflict with this plan. It may well be that the first item we recorded at ten in the morning becomes the big finish for one programme. But we need a big finish for all three of these shows, so we have to pick two other auction items that provide a suitable conclusion to a programme, then work backwards from there, positioning the rest of the available material in a way that allows that big finish to seem to emerge naturally from the mix of the individual show.

And then I arrive. What – here as well? Yes, in case you thought I took a well-earned rest while others slaved in the edit suites, at some point each programme needs my voice-over commentary – recapping people's names, objects or locations, and linking between settings where we were unable to do so on the shoot days. So I turn up in Bristol and deliver a whole lot of dialogue drafted by one or other director, which the editor then has to drop in a seamless way on to the body of the relevant programme.

After which I'm done.

Only another fifteen towns to visit for a week or so, and another series of *Flog It!* is more or less ready to air.

Don't we do well!

10

Civic Pride

I may be the holder of an as-yet-unregistered record. Yes, dear reader, I am toying with the idea of contacting the editors of the *Guinness Book of Records* to see if they might be interested in establishing a new category. And what is my territory for primacy? Where do I see my undertakings leaving all others in the shade?

Visiting town halls.

Now don't be gloomy.

Someone had to do it. And it has been me.

OK, I have not suspended myself upside down in paraffin for three minutes, single-handedly tried to cross the Alps on stilts or jumped into the lion enclosure at every British zoo and juggled lamb chops while singing a Bonnie Langford hit. My only claim to fame is striding into town halls and city halls to welcome local citizens to a *Flog It!* valuation day and welcome you, the viewers, to a new location.

That said, it is always a pleasure and a privilege.

Here I think we leave the *Antiques Roadshow* in the shade. Yes, they get to set up shop in and around stately homes every now and again, but the fact is their core venue is a stonking big sports hall, one that will accommodate at least four badminton courts. And inevitably these are essentially strictly utilitarian structures, whereas town halls are the embodiment of civic pride.

Perhaps I should write a book about them. They typically date from the 1880s to the 1920s, when Britain's towns and cities started to establish municipal facilities for the benefit of their citizens. Joseph Chamberlain was a pioneer in this respect, and Birmingham's Council House is a tribute to his desire to provide Brummies with something more than functioning drains, a satisfactory water supply, schools, hospitals and libraries.

Every city or town hall has an impressive exterior, a regal lobby and a magnificent staircase leading to the mayor's parlour and a grand function room. This is where we do some of our best *Flog It!* stuff. The night before there may have been a ball, an awards ceremony or an annual dinner in the big room. But first thing Sunday morning the ancillary staff have shifted the furniture round, and we arrive and deploy our blue cloths across a set of eight tables, and create two or more rows of chairs to provide seating accommodation for our visitors.

I generally do an introduction to the location in front of the building and in front of the queue before we head inside. This is a huge responsibility, because in a few short sentences I am determining what the afternoon viewers learn of a particular town or city: Manchester, Middlesbrough, Maidenhead, Marlborough. How do you compress their history, heritage, status and symbolism into a couple of lines? We want to convey something distinctive about each place, but we're not there to make a documentary. Nor do we simply want to reproduce the first paragraph from a tourist brochure. The *Flog It!* team anguish over this daunting task. Researchers gather facts, directors draft scripts, our producer gives them an overview and I have to believe in what's being said, and, as necessary, put it into my own words when we get to the place.

Sometimes an additional off-screen responsibility is required of me at these civic premises. I have to shake hands with the mayor. Is this because the mayor feels it is his or her duty to welcome me and the BBC to the building? Or because they want their gold chain valued? OK, here's another secret: I never ask to meet the mayor. I'm generally too concerned to do justice to the hundreds of citizens holding their belongings and shifting along the rows of seats. But frequently a mayor invites me into their parlour for a cup of tea and chat. I am made most welcome and learn that they and their family love the programme. And then I'm asked to tell them the commercial worth of the gold chain round their necks.

Mayor Joseph Chamberlain laid the foundation stone for this handsome building in Birmingham in June 1874. It was completed five years later at a cost of £163,805.

Yep, they can't resist it. And I never have a satisfactory answer, short of reminding them that such a significant artefact of local municipal heritage would never enter a commercial auction, and should the chain be superseded then its natural next home should be the local museum. If only I could persuade one of them to have the city's treasures valued by one of our experts and then put into auction. Now that would make good television. Especially if they hadn't alerted the citizens to the plan.

Mayors are a mixed bag. Most are lovely people, who have served the community as councillors for years. Some are great communicators and wonderful icons and representatives of their territories; others are less able when it comes to public relations.

Paul Martin's Britain

Leeds Corn Exchange has an extraordinary wood and glass ceiling, which did not provide quite enough light for our valuation day.

I recently had tea with the mayor of Belfast, which probably has the finest city hall we have entered. The mayoral role circulates around the political parties, including Sinn Fein. No other city hall in Britain has witnessed such dramatic and emotive swings in political fortune. Belfast's City Hall was a hundred years old in 2006 and a terrific exhibition captured a cross-section of its finest and most troubled hours.

One of our visitors brought in an old black and white photograph of the building taken from across the road on an upper floor of the famous Robinson and Cleaver department store in 1912, when thousands were gathered outside.

'What was the occasion?' I asked the owner of the panoramic picture.

'Those men were signing the Covenant,' he explained. I probably looked bemused, which isn't unusual. 'In their own blood,' he added, as if that would clarify everything. They were committing themselves to do whatever was necessary to keep Ulster part of the United Kingdom. How about that for an extraordinary vein of civic history to take on board?

Not every town has a dedicated function room alongside the mayor's offices.

Hereford's Town Hall sits opposite its Shire Hall. The latter is where the big functions are held and was the first ever venue for the *Antiques Roadshow* back in 1977. The *Roadshow* soon outgrew such limited space, but it was fine for us twenty-five years later.

The Mayor of Hereford has an office across the road from the Shire Hall. A recent incumbent was the truly stately Marcelle Lloyd-Hayes, a proud, handsome, confident woman in a big hat. She was used to the media, having just done a video diary for a

BBC West Midlands local television pilot. This had gone well, apart from when the radio microphone got caught in her underwear, and the producer had to cut it free with a Swiss army knife as she leaned over the bonnet of her limousine.

Chesterfield has the Winding Wheel. This was a cinema that was turned into a complex of beautiful function rooms in the 1980s. And we had the pleasure of occupying one of them. 'Why Winding Wheel?' we asked one of the attendants helping us prepare the room for the day. 'Because Chesterfield used to have a dozen coal mines. There was never one just here, but the name was chosen to celebrate our great industry – that was closed down by Margaret Thatcher,' this ex-miner bluntly explained.

He took us for a gang of indifferent softies from the south. But we rewrote our opening scripts for Chesterfield to acknowledge his grassroots perceptions. He had civic pride, and, one way or another, we always endeavour to acknowledge this, to highlight it and to celebrate it.

So let's hope I'm doing something useful with my visits to all these town and city halls.

And upon reflection I'm not going to write to the *Guinness Book of Records* about my achievement, because I reckon someone else may have surpassed me on this front. Now that I think about it, almost every one of those magnificent buildings has a plaque on display indicating the date when the Queen popped in.

I don't think I'd make it to the Guinness book. I fear I'd be pipped at the post by Her Majesty.

Unseasoned wood drying out too quickly in Chesterfield. The structure of the spire dried over time, causing a bending that is now treasured as a landmark.

11

Missing the Mark

Occasionally it all goes horribly wrong. I can be absolutely sure of getting a big laugh whenever I forget my lines in front of a valuation queue.

I have to walk and talk and point at the big building we are about to enter, while speaking into the camera. I have maybe fifty words to remember, in a particular order: 'Welcome to . . . home of . . . and today we're outside . . .'.

Shouldn't be too difficult, should it? Well, sometimes it isn't and sometimes it is.

Try it at home. Maybe it will roll off the tongue, or perhaps it will struggle to come out, and some key word just disappears from your consciousness. You stared at it on paper twenty times before you opened your mouth, but now it has been erased from your memory. You have no idea what this place is famous for. Was it pies, or pickles, or pottery, or plums?

This is great entertainment for those wonderful people who have kindly turned up early and are waiting patiently to enter the building. They see me for the first time in the flesh and assume I know what I am doing. So when the director says 'Action', and I start to walk and talk and halfway through I dry up or a load of absolute gibberish emerges from my lips, the crowd are amazed, then greatly amused. And, of course, that just makes it worse.

Everyone enjoys this public humiliation – apart from me and the director, who desperately wants to get on with the next shot and the next piece-to-camera.

Once inside the venue, things go relatively smoothly, though very occasionally we have a disastrous recording. People have a range of motives for wanting to sell an object via the programme. Essentially they are fed up with the thing and would prefer the cash, but sometimes they misjudge their readiness to see the object leave their lives. They tell us of that precious possession's place in family history, and suddenly they realise it means a huge amount to them. They sheepishly announce that they have changed their minds. Sometimes they phone us a few days later to tell us they have decided to hang on to it. On more than one occasion an owner has broken down in tears and wept in front of the cameras because of the emotions triggered by the object. At this point we stop the cameras, abandon that recording and gently escort the distressed owner off the premises with their now even more precious possession.

Next come the whole host of things that can go awry at the auction rooms on the day of the sale.

At home you normally see four participants in succession responding to the progress of the bidding for their object. But re-member that sometimes twenty-four items in the sale relate to our participants. That's a lot of people and objects and a lot of lots.

The auctioneers place our items about ten lots apart, so in theory we have nine other auction items that don't concern us before we need to respond to another *Flog It!* object. But all parties in front of the camera have to have a microphone tucked into their tops, so the sound man is constantly shoving cables and clips up and down people's fronts, in and out of their clothing. Then he has to check he has a clear signal from that microphone before we can proceed to film.

It's not chaos, but it seems pretty close to it at times.

The team of runners (some of whom have postgraduate media studies degrees) are ferrying in the next participant and expert to give me a chance to recollect who they are and what we are talking about. We don't always get it right, and have been known to have to do another take after the item has been sold because someone in front of the camera said the wrong thing. We occasionally forget what reserve we have put on a piece or even get someone's name wrong. Oh, the shame of it.

I am guilty of another crime: not being consistent when talking to someone about their objects. What does that mean? If a single camera is being used to film an interview, either on a valuation day or for an Insert, the director and cameraman have to undertake the recording several times. They do a wide version in which you can see both people's faces and the objects in front of them, then they do another version framing just the interviewee, then another focused on me in order to have a good picture of the question-asking. Finally they point the camera at the table-top and get shots of my hands lifting up each object in turn.

In the edit suite, they want to be able to use any angle at any time, hence the need for consistency. Unfortunately I do two things they don't like. I sometimes ask different questions the second time around – because I have thought of more aspects of the subject, or feel the interviewee will do a better job with a new, more appealing question. The professionals tell me this is generally a damned nuisance, because the second version won't work in conjunction with the first. I hereby promise, boys and girls, that I will try harder to avoid doing this.

The other thing the directors loathe is excessive handling of the objects. What they hate most is when someone at a valuation day gets out lots of things and the blue table-top is littered with objects. Remember, the director is looking ahead to the edit suite, where he has to integrate the various camera angles of the same event. The production team demand to know which objects you will be picking up and they insist that you put them down precisely in the same position.

Sounds easy, doesn't it. But when you are listening to a fascinating account of someone's family history and trying to explain to viewers the historical context of particular objects, remembering exactly where something was on the table, and at what angle, is almost impossible. Out of the corner of my eye I can see the director wincing, especially if I get into my stride with a collection of porcelain figures or toy cars.

The final area where things can go wrong is generally out of my hands. This is when our experts' estimations seriously miss the mark. Now underestimating isn't so bad, for even if the expert feels sheepish about not anticipating the interest in a particular object, the seller is so pleased with the result that the error is inconsequential. What is seriously unsatisfactory is when our expert has indicated a range of likely selling prices and the object fails miserably to hit even the bottom end of that range.

There are a number of mechanisms in place to minimise the chance of embarrassment. First on a valuation day we have four off-screen experts. Invidious though it may be for me to single out any one of them, I'll risk it. Alison Gillatt is Bonhams Regional Head of Decorative Arts, Ceramics and Oriental, no less, based in Leeds. She first helped us out when we were visiting Bradford and needed someone familiar with Asian objects. Her mum was a

Yorkshire antiques dealer and Alison went to Bonhams directly from school and has stayed there.

She diligently takes her turn at the tables and pleasantly advises owners about their objects. She's probably the best in the whole team at spotting something rare, because her knowledge and experience are so good. She'll explain to one of us what she has found and we'll then try to do it justice on screen. She's especially strong on scientific instruments, but sometimes we don't proceed with such items as we are not really confident talking

Alison Gillatt typically dealing with glassware, ceramics, jewellery and a teddy.

about them on screen. Why doesn't Alison do it herself? She took a screen test, but felt nervous and so decided she didn't want to be on telly.

So Alison and her colleagues know their stuff. We can also make a phone call to someone who has specific knowledge of a particular discipline. These days, our phone calls can include a photograph of the object in question. The production crew also keep a number of books on antiques, which come in handy for dates and places, particularly with porcelain and silverware.

Assuming we carry out a filming of a valuation, the auctioneers have the chance to make their judgements on our assessments and we generally screen them, whatever discrepancies there may be. But it has been known for an auctioneer to alert us to an error of judgement on our part, and for an item to be withdrawn from a sale because it was so far from what we thought it was worth on the valuation day. In these instances we have to discuss diplomatically with the owner what they want to happen next. Sometimes they decide to keep the item, in other cases they want it sold, but unfortunately the assessment that we made in front of the camera on the valuation day is too far removed from reality for the item to remain part of a prospective programme.

So we aim to avoid disasters, but we screen other variations between our experts' estimates and the actual selling price of an object, because that's a key element in the appeal of the programme.

First a couple of under-estimates. Audrey wanted to sell her William Wyllie seascape print. At Portsmouth James Braxton put a value of £200 on it. On the sale day in Petersfield it fetched £550. James defended his poor assessment with the well-chosen words: 'Isn't it lovely to delight the client.'

A model of a ship made in a Napoleonic prison was estimated at £400. In fact it went to £4,000, because of two phone bidders determined to demonstrate their financial virility. This was certainly not an error of estimation but simply evidence of the madness that can afflict a manic bidder. Never be one of them.

With art expert Mark Winter.

In Northern Ireland Kate Bliss estimated a Belleek plate at £300 but the owner thought it was a rare first edition worth at least £1,000. The auctioneer did not agree, but reluctantly raised the reserve to £500. At auction it reached only £360 and was withdrawn.

In Glasgow Thomas Plant valued a set of First World War medals at between £200 and £300, but a medal dealer, Geoffrey Fineman, reckoned the set was possibly a contrivance, that the medals had not necessarily belonged to one soldier and that there was no adequate provenance. The bidders at Anita Manning's sale room were not to be fooled. We had put a reserve of £150 on the medals. Anita could not get bids beyond £100 so the item was withdrawn.

At Reading Town Hall a Dutchman showed James Braxton an Austro-Hungarian silver claret jug dating from 1870 for which he had paid £1,000. James valued it at £2,000–£3,000. A few weeks later the auctioneer at Wokingham attempted to begin the bidding at £700, but no one was interested.

At Eastbourne Civic Hall Mark Stacey was impressed with an Edwin Hayes seascape, estimating it between £1,500 and £2,000. But David Holmes at the Edgar Horn auction house told me he had valued the picture a year earlier at £400–£600, and had then had to withdraw it from auction when it was found to be a fake. We felt obliged to proceed, but now had to say the painting was simply 'in the style of Edwin Hayes'. The bidders in front of our cameras took the picture to £1,350. Weird, eh?

Our experts are great companions and delightful colleagues. We rib each other at times, both on and off camera. We all take pride in doing a good job and wince whenever we miss the mark.

And, of course, there are times when it all seems so worth while. My favourite tale to date is that of Wendy Haywood of Hastings. In a local charity shop she discovered a vase that seemed rather special. She paid a few pounds for it and brought it to a *Flog It!* valuation the next day, where David Barbie confirmed it was a Clarice Cliff piece. It fetched £80 in auction and Wendy told us that she'd give all that cash back to the charity shop.

At last I've seen something I love.

12

Going, Going, Gone

ou need a big room that can hold lots of objects and has a raised lectern at one end. You require good access for the public, plus other facilities, like an office, tea and buns and a toilet.

Simple as that. It's an auction house.

But let's visit a few points on a broad spectrum. At one end we have the hallowed, elegant halls of Sotheby's and Christie's. At the far end are wooden sheds and shacks like my friend David Harrison's utilitarian Jubilee outbuilding in Pewsey. They all provide the same service: a forum to which you bring your object for evaluation and hopefully then exhibition, in order that prospective buyers can see what will be on offer at the next publicised sale day. And so decide whether or not to bid for your object. It's democratic and linear. Each object is treated entirely on its merits in the eyes of the auctioneer, not on the merits of the owner.

The auctioneer will receive a percentage of the final bid price (typically 15 per cent) and so he or she simply wants the best possible exposure for each and every item in the sale in the hope that several people at least are interested in the object and will be prepared to pursue their goals with cash. There is nothing egalitarian about the bidding process. Here ultimately money talks, and the most money takes the prize. But there is a sense that the object earns what the market will stand. This is, of course, limited by the unique circumstances of each sale: the selection of items on offer and the people who have come there to bid.

However, the results are generally fairly predictable, otherwise our *Flog It!* experts would be getting huge amounts of flak week in, week out. In fact they mostly arrive at an estimate that isn't too far from the final result.

Patently it's not predictable to the nearest pound, but in most instances they have a fairly good idea of what the market in general will stand for a particular type of item, and so what the bidding is likely to reach at a specific venue. Yes, much of the fun lies in the bidders pursuing an object in competition with each other and so pushing the selling price up, or, equally intriguing though dismaying, little interest being shown in something so that one bidder gets it at a bargain price. Remember, however, that that successful bidder has paid more for the item than anyone else in that room on that day thought it was worth.

There have always been entrepreneurs with the ability, and, generally, the premises, to organise the sale of second-hand property. In county towns this function frequently began as an adjunct to farmers' needs for trading. The farmers have sheep or cattle to sell and want the best price for their stock. An auctioneer announces the date of the sale and advertises this to prospective buyers and so the commercial worth of each animal or herd is potentially maximised. Farmers have also needed to sell or buy land and machinery. And the auctioneer would handle this, at the farm or centrally, from an office or hired hall. A death in the family is the other major trigger for a change in ownership of goods and chattels. Traditionally the eldest son would simply take over occupancy of the family home and negotiate with the rest of the family how the assets might be shared, equitably or otherwise. But some family circumstances would mean property was no longer required. The quickest and most fruitful means of transforming those items into cash was to put them into the hands of a local auctioneer, who would in turn bring them to the attention of everyone in the area. One person gets rid of a possession in exchange for cash. Another transacts cash for that object. Auctioneer gets a percentage. Everyone happy. That's the process in a nutshell.

In today's complex, fast-moving, mobile, fashion-oriented world, the appetite for auctions is big, and so auction houses are found in most towns and cities, most of them dealing with a very broad range of items. Only the exceptional and the best are worth carting off to London for examination by the big houses, who have a bidding clientele interested in and capable of purchasing the very best examples in each field. Traditionally Sotheby's, Christie's and Bonhams have handled the elite for the elite, and, while anyone is welcome

Something that caught my eye was this nineteenth-century ex-frame chair, in the Italian manner, and this time it was my turn to be the expert.

inside those grand houses, they retain an air of mannered money; big on etiquette, short on egalitarianism. I've enjoyed visiting these places for many years, getting my eyes and hands on wonderful examples of every type of furniture, then seeing what those pieces will fetch from a group of buyers for whom economy is not everything.

There are well-heeled people who roam the prime auction houses on a regular basis. It's a sort of rich person's hobby. They call it 'doing the rooms'. Alongside them are the canny types who are in the trade. They are attempting to spot something that they can take away and mark up for their own clientele, people who wouldn't have the time or inclination to hang around for the best part of a day waiting to try their luck on a single object without any idea whether their interest will be outmatched by someone with a deeper pocket.

This was all a rather closed world until the television industry hit on the dramatic appeal of witnessing the auction process, and monitoring the financial gain that resulted from spotting the worth of an undervalued item and getting it to a buyer with the appetite and capacity to pay handsomely. BBC television's *Lovejoy* drama series woke Britain up overnight to the appreciation of old artefacts and to the people who earned a living negotiating for and manoeuvring those objects towards customers with plenty of cash.

Ian McShane was great as the central character. People have asked if he was based on a real trader. To the best of my knowledge the answer is no. However, people say I remind them of Lovejoy. I assume that this notion is based primarily on my hairstyle. I seem to remember that Lovejoy was occasionally undertaking questionable transactions with dodgy objects and mysterious middle-men. He was what would be called a 'divvy' in the trade, operating on the fringes of legitimacy and delivering objects into the mainstream that hadn't exactly been stolen, but perhaps had a questionable provenance. I don't believe I've ever done anything whose legitimacy might keep me awake at night.

When *Flog It!* visited East Anglia, I was asked by the producer to make reference to the Lovejoy legend. I agreed, and so they found an open-topped Morris Minor for me to drive past the front of 'Bellsham Hall', the home of 'Lady Jane' in the village of Long Melford, where the series was filmed.

The other big figure who dragged the antiques world centre-stage on television was David Dickinson, another man with long locks, like me and Lovejoy. David was responsible for BBC1's *Bargain Hunt*, a programme that fascinated people and could be said to have started it all. He was at the high end of the business, but not out of the public-school mould, demonstrating that anyone with enthusiasm, intelligence, passion and flair could work fruitfully in the field.

All the popular daytime collectables programmes rely on a stable of antiques experts, most of whom are regional auctioneers, either those running their own businesses or key employees in a bigger concern. This is why they are so good at knowing what things are and what they are likely to be worth. All credit to my old boss Mark Hill for identifying and nurturing this territory as the potential basis for fascinating programmes.

These are my tips on technique for happy hunting at your average auction house:

'Before the sale, let's see what the auctioneer has to say about some of our owners' items.'

● Visit on preview day and examine the objects immensely carefully. If there's something you want to know, ask one of the staff. Most houses issue a listing of estimates. Sometimes these are printed up within the catalogue; occasionally it's just a single copy of the catalogue with scribbled estimates in the margins.

● If you are going to turn up and bid, then your preview visit is a good time to register. The house needs your details and can give you a bidding card with a unique number on it. You can just stick your hand up on a whim on the day without being registered, but the auctioneer prefers to know there is a record for that person, and it just helps the event go smoothly.

● If you can't make the auction day, you can arrange to leave a maximum bid that will be deployed by the auctioneer depending on what's happening on the floor when that item goes under the hammer. He or she will incrementally use your bid to advance the sale. They should not jump to your top figure but allow the bidding to head towards that ceiling, and let it naturally stop where the market determines. Alternatively you can arrange a phone line. One of the auction house team will ring you so you can monitor the bidding and add to it as far as you wish.

● If you're on the floor of the auction house on the day, don't fan yourself with your catalogue. Auctioneers are immensely sharp at recognising a serious bidder rather than someone who's just scratching their nose, though some serious and discreet bidders do little more than scratch their noses and the auctioneer knows exactly what they mean.

● Please don't wander through the auction talking loudly like Yours Truly does when winding up a programme. Our venues are immensely accommodating of us, but it would be completely against good practice for visitors to adopt anything other than a low profile while the auctioneer is wielding that gavel.

- The auction firms like you to remove your purchases from their premises on the day of the sale. Some will give you a couple of days' grace. If it's furniture, you may require help in lifting. They have porters available – to take your purchase to a suitable vehicle with suitable insurance.

- Remember you will pay the selling price, plus the auctioneer's premium, plus VAT on top of that. Unless you are going to pay in cash, the auction house will want to be able to verify your credit worthiness. Some will accept credit or debit cards, others won't.

- If you find that your object is not as it was described in the catalogue, you can return it and seek a full refund within fourteen days.

The production team, filming auctioneers' chat.

A couple of factors have hugely changed the auction landscape in the last decade. First the disappearance of your average American from UK shores. Britain was a top holiday destination for Americans, who came for lightning tours of little old England: a coach ride past Buckingham Palace, zip up to Stratford for a flavour of Shakespeare country, then it's souvenir time. And the wealthy ones didn't just want a translucent plastic dome in which fake snow falls in slow motion over a crude model of Big Ben. They wanted genuine British antiques. So they lifted the market and injected interest and income into the trade. But those days are gone. Since 9/11, Americans have become much more insular, disinclined to fly over to Europe for a gadabout.

Paul Martin's Britain

Putting the auctioneer on the spot.

The other landscape-changing factor has opened up trade as opposed to narrowing horizons. This is the Internet. Now every auction house from Sotheby's downwards can alert potential customers of every interesting proposition. And, in parallel, the highly democratic phenomenon known as eBay allows anyone to be a trader from the comfort of their own home. So technology has vastly expanded the sources and the bidders for every object. And the range of items being offered for sale is continuing to grow. Occasionally American auctions include items that have travelled through space. Yes, somehow the contents of NASA shuttles are available to buy. Someone recently picked up a mission emblem patch that had travelled in Apollo X for $4,000.

Traditionalists say there is no substitute for getting your eyes and hands on the object in question. They point out you won't fall in love with a photograph, neither will you spot the tiny flaw that the camera hides. In theory Internet traders are obliged to alert viewers to any shortcomings in the object being sold. But whether you're buying a Victorian Royal Worcester pot or a pair of second-hand designer jeans, not until you look at and feel your purchase can you be sure it's something you really want.

Going, Going, Gone

So I don't think traditional auction houses are about to disappear, though there is some rationalisation by bigger players, buying up smaller houses and branding the rooms under their trading name, then shifting objects between locations to establish centres for particular types of sale.

I've occasionally undertaken bidding in front of the camera, perhaps most memorably in Colchester at the Reeman, Dansie and Howe rooms, where I took a fancy to an eighteenth-century elm dresser, for which I told viewers I was prepared to pay a maximum of £900. The bidding started at £400, and I swiftly became aware of two phone bidders having their contributions brought to the auctioneer's attention. I made a couple of stabs but the bidding was soon at £900 and heading upwards. Despite my declared ceiling, I now went on and bid further. How foolish is this? Had I set my heart on the object, and so lost my head? I bid £1,100, but it didn't stay there and moved onwards and upwards. I got a grip of myself and didn't stick my hand up again. The final phone bid was £1,300, definitely more than I think the item was worth before restoration.

I hope the outcome was a useful demonstration of the bidding process: the emotions, financial roller-coaster ride and swift decision-making in the light of rapidly changing circumstances. That's the fun of auctions, if you have the stomach and wallet for it. Perhaps I made a fool of myself, but my hope is that it left everyone wiser.

If you've never visited an auction, see it as a couple of fascinating days out that don't have to cost you a penny. But beware: there's a tiny chance you might be elbowed into the aisles by a crazy camera crew trying to record a critical link by Yours Truly without completely destroying the atmosphere and auction for sensible visitors.

13

Bluebell Blues

Back in the early days of *Flog It!*, when I was trying to get a handle on what the commitment to being on television every day entailed, I was sure I could continue to travel around the country with my German Shepherd pup, Bluebell, in tow. That's not the right term, because she was never in tow, she was always simply my companion, sometimes on her lead, but often not. She had travelled with me to auctions all over the place, guarding my car and keeping me fit. No reason why she shouldn't enjoy a similar role while I did a few pieces-to-camera or interviews. Well, she had a damned good go at it. And in the early days, she appeared in valuation days and on Insert items. Auction house interiors were a no-no, of course. A wagging tail in the vicinity of precious porcelain is beyond the pale.

Paul Martin's Britain

Bluebell couldn't be left at home by herself all day long, so she has a new companion. Her new best friend and the latest addition to the household is Diesel, a rescue Bassett, named by his first owners after the action movie hero Vin Diesel. It was only after a while that we saw the likeness: the big chest and the small bum! The name has stuck.

So those early programmes show me and Blue doing *Flog It!* And once they were transmitted, then people expected to see me with my beautiful German Shepherd, and I had no wish to let them down. But the practicalities started to become a problem.

Unlike the old days when I could pop out to Blue whenever necessary, to give her a walk or just a good cuddle, now I was surrounded by anxious directors concerned to get sufficient footage in the can hour by hour, day by day, so they had the makings of complete programmes to edit back in Bristol. Me popping out to air or water my pet ran against the grain of a working day on the road in the television industry.

Blue was never a problem in hotels, and in most cases the establishments were prepared to make arrangements that would allow her a roof over her head for the night. But the fact is a dog likes its own territory, and doesn't want to be under a different roof night after night. The more shows the BBC wanted me to do, the less practical it was for Blue to accompany me. I had to make a big and painful compromise. I took Blue down to Falmouth to live with my mum during the week. I would go down there and bring her back home on those weekends when I wasn't doing a Sunday valuation.

For a while the BBC even put a few shots of Blue in the opening titles. This was the programme presented by the bloke with a dog. Well, it stopped being presented by the bloke and the dog, and became the programme presented just by the bloke. So they took Blue out of the titles, but the sense of my owning and loving that animal has stayed with my public persona, and I seldom go anywhere without people asking me 'Where's your dog?', 'How's your dog?' or 'Where's Blue?'. Of course every time someone kindly asks one of these questions, I am abruptly reminded of the fact she's not with me, and I'm missing her. And I imagine she's missing me, too.

When there was a valuation day in Exeter recently I decided to take Blue along for old times' sake. When I entered the venue with Blue at my side, people started clapping and this swiftly built to a huge round of applause from the pleasure everyone got at seeing the bloke's dog. It brought a big lump to my throat, and, while I can't speak for her, I imagine Blue felt much the same.

14

So Many Strange Beds

During the last few years I have spent on average 220 nights in hotels per year. Admittedly good ones, and some amazing ones – Bovey Castle on Dartmoor, Stapleford Park in Melton Mowbray and a real delight, Hotel Tresanton in St Mawes, Cornwall, with probably the best cuisine in the country – but nevertheless the majority still represent strange beds in strange places and unfamiliar bathrooms. As people who spend a lot of time on the road will always tell you, the novelty soon wears off. What would be a treat for a holiday becomes a fag. I know many businessmen who wish they could spend more time in their own beds and I feel the same.

The bands I was in never had enough money for good hotels. We roughed it, but I was younger then. I guess the groups that

Paul Martin's Britain

Filming just down the road at Avebury. No strange bed required.

become successful and can afford big hotel bills do then face the same regime of the strange bed in a strange place. But their daily pattern is different. They will probably sit around in the bedroom during the afternoon, then go do their work in the evening. They doubtless get back late and enjoy a drink or three, and/or some other relaxing activity, before going to bed well after midnight knowing they can have a lie-in.

However, the businessmen and I always have to be up bright and early. So I operate a strict system in the evenings. I endeavour to eat by 7.30 p.m. to give my supper time to settle. I will have a beer, or a couple of glasses of wine, but no more.

Now some of my female fans really don't believe this. I generally go to bed at about ten o'clock and read my notes or scripts relating to tomorrow's tasks. I am not out on the razzle – or in on the razzle for that matter – as I make my way around the country, hotel by hotel by hotel. If I were to get drunk and disorderly in the evenings, it would inevitably show on my face the next day, and the cameraman would be stuck with a rough-looking presenter unable to remember his lines. The fact is, I'm not a night bird; I go to bed early to make the day go more quickly. I miss Charlotte and home.

Oh marvellous days and nights when *Flog It!* came to Marlborough while I was living there. The crew were assigned to the Castle and Ball on the high street, a delightful hotel with a wonderful coaching inn heritage. I invited them all to my flat for a drink, which is something I am seldom able to do. We had supper in Coles, a great restaurant just up the road from my old shop, where they know how to look after you while putting on a great spread. For me, it is simply the best restaurant in Wiltshire. Then I went back home and slept in my own bed. What novelty.

Next morning, no Graham, no car. I walked a couple of hundred yards from my front door to the Merchant's House for our first Insert recording. Built in 1653 following the great fire of Marlborough, this is my ideal environment, a glorious example of a handsome town dwelling full of fabulous oak and period furnishings. I did toy with inviting the crew back for lunch at my place, but I feared it would take too long, and so we had our usual hurried café jacket potatoes before setting off to Avebury for the afternoon. The highlight of this Insert was my meeting with a genuine Druid, who explained, then demonstrated, how he called up the spirits of the Solstice.

With two extremely different aspects of our heritage in the can, it was back to my own flat in time to watch the teatime news. That's my idea of a perfect working day.

Paul Martin's Britain

Home from home: the Peacock.

Look out for the carved mice!

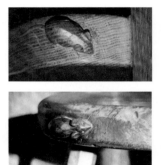

There's a fascinating game in the bar that dates back to the early 1800s. While you're waiting for your pint to be pulled, can you balance all six nails on one vertical?

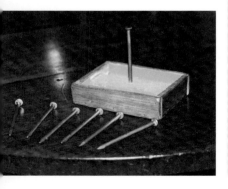

One of my favourite hotels, from which I can reach a wide range of locations across the north Midlands, is the Peacock at Rowsley on the A6 north of Matlock. It was built as a manor house in 1652 and was part of the estate of Lord Manners of Haddon Hall. The reception rooms and bedrooms are lovely, and contain lots of fine furniture. There is a scatter of smashing 'Mousey' Thompson tables and chairs with their signature little carved mice in the bar. But best of all is an extraordinary chair that has a special right-hand arm with a small circular table-top built into it. I've never seen one like it.

The bar and restaurant offer great food. Matthew the chef even gave me a cooking lesson early one evening, and I helped cook my own sea bass supper. Nothing like passing down the skills of the trade. And why is he so good? Well, he's been trained by Gordon Ramsey.

Apparently the manor house was often occupied by a formidable Victorian fisherman, George Butcher, who knew every inch of the adjacent River Wye, and could catch a trout better than

This eighteenth-century chair was made for the person overseeing cock fighting. He would take the bets, and the stakes would be laid out on the tray incorporated into the arm. Nowadays it's a perfect drinking accessory: somewhere to put your pint.

It took me weeks to do this, but I don't mind sharing the answer with you

anyone. I am no great fisherman, but I have occasionally had a go when I've had a few hours to spare between shoots. It's a great way to relax, even if I achieve nothing. The Wye is the only river in England where wild rainbow trout breed naturally. The fishing is carefully monitored and is strictly 'catch and release'.

15

Hurrah for the National Trust

I'm not a scholar. University of life, plus occasional knocks, that's me, whereas the *Antiques Roadshow* experts are mostly art history graduates, chaps who didn't want to join the civil service or be something in the City. But I did get one heck of an education in art history – thanks to my mum, my dad and the National Trust.

Most weekends I was taken by my parents to one of the Trust's properties and would spend the day examining buildings inside and out, quizzing the guides and reading the booklets. I have visited every Trust property in Devon and Cornwall at least once, several half a dozen times. And I've been to a cross-section of the Trust places across the country, which stood me in very good stead when I started to trade on Portobello Market. I could

Paul Martin's Britain

The National Trust offers not just an educational day, but a fun day out.

identify different woods and recognise the quality of furniture making and the finish of furnishings. That's where I did my hands-on bit.

The National Trust came to life in 1895 when a trio of Victorian philanthropists decided to preserve some threatened buildings, gardens and coastline from the relentless advance of economic development. They began by acquiring and thus protecting the garden at Sayes Court in Deptford. Now the Trust looks after half a million acres, including 200 buildings and gardens and 700 miles of coastline. The structures range from castles to pubs, and all of them are presented tastefully and intelligently. Every Trust property guarantees an enlightening experience.

Hurrah for the National Trust

So thank you, National Trust – because I think there can be no better education than to steep oneself in the magnificent array of properties the charity has so carefully, enjoyably and respectfully brought under its broad wing.

If it wasn't for the National Trust, we wouldn't have such dramatic backdrops for filming *Flog It!* in locations all over the country. Here I'm at Fountains Abbey in Yorkshire. It offers a sense of connection to the past and inspiration for the future.

16

Pictures of Britain

I greatly enjoyed David Dimbleby's BBC1 series *A Picture of Britain*, looking at landscapes, who had painted them and how.

Inexplicably he didn't ask me to help him with those programmes, because, in our ever modest way, we have tackled much of the same territory on *Flog It!* Albeit taking a lot of detours en route, we have travelled the country, visiting art galleries, examining the sites of some great paintings and learning about the artists.

As with all aspects of *Flog It!*, this has been a great pleasure.

Let's start in the Midlands with a timeless subject given a contemporary treatment. David Dimbleby invested time in wandering the Malvern Hills in Worcestershire, mostly listening to

Paul Martin's Britain

The Malvern Hills, a 7-mile ridge of granite, brilliantly captured in his paintings by David Prentice.

passages of Edward Elgar's music, and why not, indeed? The Malverns' ridge rises dramatically and abruptly out of the Severn plain. It's a surge of granite running north–south, splitting Worcestershire from Herefordshire and producing a massive silhouette for each of those counties as the day proceeds and the sun casts its shadow from one side and then the other.

Unlike most hills, where, when you get to the top, you are looking down on smaller hills, on top of the Malverns you are looking down at small towns or farmers' fields. It's like being in a light aircraft. They are wonderful to walk, and one can understand why the great composer got his inspiration for 'Land of Hope and Glory' striding along these noble rises.

But the Malverns are very difficult to photograph. As you move along you constantly appreciate their shape and impact. But stop and look through a lens, and you don't have the whole picture. No single frame can do the job. Cue a painter.

David Prentice has spent years wandering the hills and capturing their beauty. He continues to work and deliver wonderful results. The Cowleigh Gallery has always been a showcase for his work, though perhaps his finest images of the hills are those purchased by the West Mercia Constabulary for their headquarters at Hindlip Hall. Sadly these are inaccessible to the general public – unless you are helping the police with their enquiries, of course, when you will probably have other things on your mind than attractive landscapes.

Admiring work in progress, in David Prentice's studio.

Paul Martin's Britain

Norman Cornish, *Bust Bara*, oil on canvas.

Now let's head up to Salford to look up L.S. Lowry. The Lowry on Salford Quays celebrates the man who made the iconic matchstick men most honourably. Something the Dimbleby tour didn't take in is the fact that Lowry's old house in Salford still stands – halfway down a busy high street. Because of its location – behind a short garden and close to double yellow lines – the council doesn't publicly acknowledge it, as visitors would create a traffic problem and there's nowhere nearby to park. If the man had had a swanky residence in the country, it would probably by now be a National Trust or English Heritage visitor centre. Because he worked as a rent collector in a working-class community, capturing that community on canvas brilliantly and distinctively in his spare time, the dwelling in which he undertook his work while looking after his sickly mother remains sadly anonymous.

Next let's venture further north to Tyneside for some more working-class art.

I spent a fascinating day with Norman Cornish not long ago. He was a coal miner in Durham who sketched in his spare time. He created landscapes, buildings and representations of his colleagues and friends. He reckoned he could make a living at it and so packed in mining, and I am pleased to report that his instincts were correct. His paintings now fetch between £4,000 and £12,000.

Heading down the east coast brings us to Yorkshire and the Staithes School – capturing the challenging work of fishermen and women. Staithes was an isolated little fishing port, with more than a smattering of foreigners who had arrived by boat and decided to stay. It was cut off from the rest of the country until the coming of the railway – then it became an attractive place for tourists. Some were artists fascinated by the distinctive nature of the buildings, scattered on the hills above the harbour. This was towards the end of the nineteenth century, and some of these painters were eager to get away from the traditional upper-class horse-and-hounds subject matter and instead tackle ordinary people working for a living. Some of these new-wave painters were also influenced by the French impressionists. Frederick Jackson was probably foremost in the group and made a significant impression in the art world. He could have left Yorkshire to be feted by the London galleries, but instead stayed around Staithes and laboured at his art for many years until illness overcame him. He turned to teaching, and among his pupils were Laura Johnson and her future husband Harold Knight, both of whom later moved to Cornwall. Laura Knight was made a Dame in 1929 and in 1936 became the first woman elected to the Royal Academy. During the Second World War she was an official war artist and produced many haunting, sobering images of the battlefields and their aftermath.

The painter Cornish. I'm just in love with this man's work, and one day I will own some.

105

Paul Martin's Britain

Mark Senior, *Toil*, oil on canvas.

I had a chance to go Flatford Mill and stand on the spot where Constable captured *The Hay-Wain* in 1821. This is a very different England from that of Lowry. Here all is in harmony – agriculture responds to the seasons, the land provides for the people. But that stable hierarchy of rural life was on the brink of being fractured as Constable pursued his craft – thanks to the Industrial Revolution, mechanisation would impact on farming methods. Machines were about to appear over the horizon that would work the land and its crops and so replace the body of workers in their humble cottages who for generations had dutifully underpinned the needs of the big landowners at harvest time.

Fewer farm workers were required. Those without work would move to the cities to toil in the noisy, dirty, smoke-filled, soul-destroying factories. Their descendants would be the subjects of Lowry's brush – thin, bent creatures scuttling from the mill to their tiny terraced houses, short of light, food, fulfilment and greenery.

John Constable's work found a ready audience almost as soon as the canvas was dry. He appealed to a Romantic vision of the countryside: a place of order, stability, balance and aesthetic joy.

Many artists jumped aboard this fruitful bandwagon and pursued the capture of idyllic rural scenes, of which many versions were available. These artists were mostly minnows, swimming in the wake of Constable's great white shark. But some were more cunning creatures who didn't simply ape Constable's technique but tried to pass off paintings as those of the great man, complete with forged signature.

These attempts to produce pretend Constables trickled along for a century, then up popped Tom Keating. Here was an extremely able artist who could attract only modest interest in his own original efforts. But if he painted in the style of Constable, he could quickly find someone willing to pay far more for the picture. When he placed Constable's signature in the corner, the commercial value jumped enormously. There was always someone drifting around with more money than sense who would write a cheque for something they were told was a little-known, recently discovered Constable.

Keating saw this as a golden vein. Even though people would not be queuing up to own a Keating, his work was in demand – impeccable forgeries of Constable. In the 1950s he turned this into a one-man industry, and the legitimate art world was somewhat slow in spotting that fakes were peppering the borders of their business. Other artists saw Keating's commercial success, and they too jumped on *The Hay-Wain*, to make hay while the sun seemed to shine.

Eventually Keating was caught and exposed, and actually jailed for his deceptions. His legacy has been a permanent degree of confusion over the legitimacy of work in the Constable mould.

At Colchester auction rooms art expert Mark Winter explained to me the comparative valuations of paintings attributed to John Constable. First he pointed out the tell-tale signs of forgery and would-be downright deception. Some paintings that are passed of as Constables have actually been manufactured in the Far East – by machine. The stuff on the surface of what seems to be canvas is not oil paint at all but a synthetic substance that adds texture to a print. In Colchester, if they see fit to sell a picture that looks like a Constable, they may well refer to it as 'after the artist', acknowledging that it is a legitimate attempt to reflect the style of the master. The term 'school of' places the picture as having come from those artists who worked with and around Constable and who may have been required by Constable to undertake a piece that could be sold as his original work. 'Attributed to' is a further stage along the scale, where the evidence would suggest that Constable himself did most of the work, but it may have been finished off by an apprentice.

Is there money in copies and fakes? Yes.

Keating's copies change hands for £10,000 these days. Other copies without a false signature can also make this figure. Paintings described as 'school of' can make £30,000 to £40,000. Those attributed to Constable come in at £100,000, and a true Constable – immensely unlikely to emerge from an attic with a hundred years' dust on it – will fetch £200,000 or more.

I once made a stab at owning a tiny relic of Constable's œuvre. I am sent lots of catalogues by auction houses, probably because they are hoping this might encourage *Flog It!* to use them as a venue. In a Somerset auction house catalogue I noticed an original Constable painting for sale. Why hadn't this been taken to Sotheby's so the big boys could fight over it? Because it was just a couple of inches square, and was painted not on canvas but on tin. The lid of a tobacco tin, to be precise. A flaky painting of a cow by a barn. Nevertheless this was a Constable. It was a present for his nephew, done quickly as a birthday gift for the 12-year-old.

It was valued in the catalogue at between £3,000 and £6,000. I decided I would invest in this tiny fragment of the genius's portfolio and alerted the auction house to my top bid of £5,500. This didn't sustain me for more than a few seconds on the day. I was outbid almost immediately and the precious tobacco tin left Crewkerne with a price tag of £12,000.

It is extraordinary to think that Constable and Turner vied for attention at the Royal Academy for several years. Each would add a dab to their submissions at the last moment to try to upstage the other.

Joseph Mallord William Turner became the youngest ever member of the Royal Academy at the age of 26 in 1802. Not bad for a lad whose dad worked as a barber in Covent Garden. Turner spent the next fifty years diligently producing the most impressive and exquisitely beautiful body of work. He didn't simply confine himself to one area and one style. This artistic giant covered Britain, then traversed Europe, capturing landscapes, buildings, objects, people and most of all light, with staggering effect.

The good news is almost every library in the land has at least a few books on Turner and a great one to begin with is Olivier Meslay's pocket guide. If you can, spend a day at Tate Britain and absorb Turner's magnificent body of work – or if you cannot get there in person, go electronically to www.tate.org.uk.

Halfway between Brighton and Eastbourne is one of my favourite houses, a seventeenth-century farmhouse, converted into a magically absorbing honeypot of glorious decoration and design by two of the key figures from the Bloomsbury Group.

This was a loose alliance of clever, privileged, artistic figures who meandered between family homes and studios in London, trips to the capitals and galleries of Europe and seasons at the seaside, doing bits of painting, posing and pontificating.

Vanessa Bell and Duncan Grant set up home at Charleston near the village of Berwick, not far from Lewes. And the rest of the flock soon drifted in for short or long stays. They cross-fertilised each other both intellectually and artistically. Allegedly sexually, too, in a number of instances.

They painted, wrote and designed, and applied their talent to the interior of the building with extraordinary vigour and confidence to make it a unique place. In terms of a contemporary equivalent, the best comparison I can come up with is the Monty Python gang, or the Young Ones team. With the arrival of the television industry, collectives of like-minded performers had a potential platform for their talent. The allegiances established at

A visit to Charleston House makes you want to get your paint brush out and paint every surface.

Oxford, Cambridge or Manchester could be continued at the BBC at White City, and each individual could contribute his or her style and character to the collective pot. In a somewhat similar way, Charleston is a tribute to the endeavours of an impressive collective. The big names associated with the gang are the writer Virginia Woolf, her sister Vanessa Bell and John Maynard Keynes, the respected early twentieth-century economist.

Simon Jenkins includes Charleston in his formidable *England's Thousand Best Houses*: 'We must imagine Bells and Grants wandering round in smocks, perpetually dabbing paint on walls, cupboards, doors, chairs, anything that caught their eye.' That sounds a tad cynical, but he then adds: 'Charleston makes us want to look afresh at our own homes, wondering how a touch of the paintbrush might bring them more to life.'

Television has certainly delivered us colossal amounts of information and advice about what we could and should do with our houses, with the deployment of MDF and decking enjoying particularly high status, but to date pottering about with a paintbrush has not been much recommended. Check out Charleston. It might change your views.

Along the south coast, we can fruitfully make Portsmouth a port of call. Heading into the harbour, we will notice a fine

Georgian house on the east side of the estuary. This was the home of William Wyllie, a marine artist who produced a formidable collection of sketches of English coastal ships and shipping in the early part of the twentieth century. His most frequently seen work is the marvellous panorama of the Battle of Trafalgar that occupies pride of pace in an audio-visual gallery at the Naval Dockyards. It's 3 metres high and 14 metres long. Robert Perera runs a gallery at Lymington devoted to Wyllie's work. You can pick up a signed print from £400.

Let's finish my instant tour of the English painting world in the West Country.

It would seem many a painter has taken heed of the instruction 'Go west, young man' (or woman), because the number of artists who saw fit to travel to Cornwall and stay is considerable.

Flog It! has dipped into a range of the galleries and schools that constitute this vibrant, evolving community. At the Penlee House Gallery in Penzance Alison Bevan showed me two classic images of the Newlyn School that draw appreciative visitors from all over the world.

Elizabeth Armstrong was born in Canada and studied art in Europe, then heard of a new colony of artists gathering in Cornwall. She came to have a look and met Stanhope Forbes (1857–1947) and they married a few years later. Stanhope was an Irishman who had discovered Newlyn in 1884 and swiftly gained national recognition with his *Fish Sale on a Cornish Beach* at the Royal Academy a year later. In the year of their marriage, 1889, the Forbes set up a school of painting, and this attracted in a new generation of artists.

In this same year, Elizabeth produced her most celebrated picture, *School is Out*. She later wrote and illustrated a children's book entitled *King Arthur's Wood*, which was very popular with middle-class Edwardian children.

Paul Martin's Britain

The Forbes had one child, Alec. Elizabeth died just before the First World War and Alec was killed in it. Stanhope continued to paint in the area until the Second World War. I sometimes come across people who remember as children gazing at the easel of this talented elderly gentleman.

It was the light that drew the artists to the area. The granite sand reflected the sunlight, which gave landscapes and seascapes a crispness that was intriguing to capture.

Elizabeth Forbes, *School is Out*.

Ironically, Penlee's most popular painting features a downpour. Norman Garstin, another Irishman drawn to the area, reached Newlyn in 1886 and moved into Penzance in 1889. His image of umbrella-carrying figures on a rainswept promenade, *The Rain It Raineth Every Day*, is one of the world's favourites.

I hope this sketch of a few elements in my perceptions of favourite paintings and painters is interesting. Join the dots and gain the bigger picture. I'm not much of a painter myself, whereas I understand that David Dimbleby is pretty good. I would be only too happy to follow in his footsteps.

Norman Garstin, *The Rain It Raineth Every Day*.

17

Seeing Sculpture

I have little appetite for sharks in formaldehyde or heaps of bricks representing something other than a building site within the walls of a gallery, but that doesn't mean I don't enjoy contemporary sculpture – as long as it seems to have a legitimate aesthetic function.

Sometime in the twentieth century sculptors moved away from attempts to capture accurately the pose and expressions of their human subjects and instead began to indicate a character and attitude with bold, expressive lines and shapes.

Shame, I say.

The traditional work was generally undertaken in stone or cast in bronze. Since the demise of realism, there have been determined efforts to exploit new materials. One that is in

The Willow Man in Somerset.

harmony with its setting is the Willow Man who stands north of Bridgwater in Somerset between the M5 and the Exeter–Plymouth railway line. You can't miss him. He was erected by Serena de la Hey, then re-erected by her after he was set on fire by vandals. The second time around Serena stuck him on a small island, which she had had created in a farmer's field. Essentially a moat has been dug around the fellow, making him much less susceptible to fire.

Willow is a valuable crop from the Somerset levels. Black maul is used specifically for weaving. The resultant rods, a couple of metres long, can be used with the bark intact or stripped off to give the willow a smoother finish. The Willow Man is a modern Green Man, the character in folklore who heralded health for the harvest. The medieval Green Man was a spirit who looked over and after the farm and its fruits. Serena has celebrated those traditions in a stylish fashion for fast-moving travellers, bringing right up to date the principle of placing a sculpture or statue in a public place – at the side of a road, or even in the middle of a road, or on a roundabout.

Is a supermarket car park a good place for sculpture? To the east of Darlington, just off the A66, is yet another Morrisons, but a Morrisons with a difference, because it's the only branch of the retail chain to have a life-size representation of a railway loco-motive made out of brick alongside. The Stockton–Darlington Railway of 1825 pioneered steam locomotion, and, to celebrate this, the Department of National Heritage invited Scottish sculptor David Mach to create an impression of the *Mallard* setting the 1938 steam locomotive speed record (of 126 mph) with bricks, 185,000 of them. For the record they are Accrington Nori bricks, and thirty-four brickies took twenty-one weeks to assemble the 60-metre long, 6-metre high structure. It certainly takes your mind off the shopping, but I wonder if there might not have been a better location for this fine piece. Outside Darlington station perhaps?

Adding to the civic pride of Tyneside is this spectacular Millennium footbridge, sculpture at its most functional.

Paul Martin's Britain

Barbara Hepworth.
Seeing her work is seeing
sculpture.

Anthony Gormley climbed aboard the roadside bandwagon when he commenced his *Angel of the North* at the side of the Great North Road, south of Gateshead. This was a challenging endeavour, not naturally at one with the landscape it occupies. It's certainly powerful and seen by millions of passers-by, but it's far from being universally treasured. It was commissioned by Gateshead Council, who managed to persuade the Arts Council of England and the European Regional Development Fund to support it. £584,000 of the cost came from the National Lottery. Locals were incensed that this money was not being spent on schools and hospitals in the area. However, a councillor pointed out that more than this had been spent by locals on lottery tickets, so his constituents really had nothing to complain about. For those who don't know, it's made of prerusted steel, weighs 100 tons and is 65 feet high with a wingspan of 175 feet.

Not all of Sir Anthony's work gets such a high profile. I was enchanted to come across one of his most obscure pieces. It's of a woman halfway up a cliff-face in a disused quarry in Dorset where I went on a sculpting course. I spent four days being schooled in techniques for satisfyingly hacking at a hunk of limestone and finding something inside, or something inside me. The process requires energy and a dynamic, and is a very absorbing experience. If you feel down in the dumps, I can recommend stone sculpting. It brings out the best in you. You discover things about yourself. It's got soul.

My favourite modern sculptor is Barbara Hepworth, whose garden and museum at St Ives in Cornwall are sympathetically tended by the Tate. Take time to look at the work there, then return to see it in a different light. Literally. This was a vital aspect of her perceptions of the capacity of the modern sculpted form: its ability to move with the sun and clouds. Her son was killed in an aircraft accident in 1953, shortly after her marriage had broken up. She continued to work with flair and fortitude from her St Ives haven. She was diagnosed with cancer in 1964 and made a Dame Commander of the British Empire a year later. Despite being confined to a wheelchair, she pursued her work in a simple, even primitive fashion. Ten years later she died in a fire in her studio.

A wonderful woman, with a wonderful body of work. See it, and see sculpture.

18

Working with Wood

A favourite place of mine is the National Arboretum at
Westonbirt, just south of Prince Charles's Highgrove
estate near Tetbury. Its 600 acres offer the endless
pleasure of wandering among 18,000 trees and shrubs. The park
is the legacy of a wealthy Victorian, Robert Holford, who, as a bit
of a hobby, decided to gather at least one good example of every
tree he could get his hands on.

By that I don't mean he got his hands dirty, or even went very
far in search of new specimens. He had others to do the dirty
work for him. Robert had the money to pay for it. Many an
expedition that set out by ship to faraway places anticipated
selling a plant or three to Robert when they got back. As well as
money, he seemed to have had good taste in design, or at least he

Once the tree is felled, it is sawn through to season naturally and to reduce its moisture content.

had the wisdom to employ people with good taste. So the estate is delightfully landscaped and the trees are planted in eye-catching clusters. He and his team must have simply guessed at how the end result would look, because it's only now, 150 years later, that those efforts have fully come to fruition.

Among the softwoods, or evergreens, look out for the red cedars that were a vital asset for the early American settlers, allowing them to build canoes, carts and houses. Curiously, its foliage has a smell that reminds me, and others, of pineapples.

Dutch elm disease killed 30 million examples of that wonderful tree back in the 1970s. A few survived in Brighton and on the Scilly Isles and at Westonbirt. The elm was a favourite for chair-makers, as its grain has a density and weave that allows it to withstand shock.

Another furniture-maker's valued raw material was the yew, which lends itself to turning and steam-bending, and hence can have a key role in sturdy chair construction. Yews are often found in churchyards and have frequently been there far longer than the church itself. The yew continues to grow for, would you believe, 2,000 years. Then the root system starts to pull apart. The heart-wood becomes exposed and is weathered, and this produces a hollow down the middle of the trunk. Frequently a branch falls down that central cavity and it rests in the base and then begins to produce roots. A new yew starts to form inside the body of the old; hence the tree renews itself and so seems to possess immortality.

Its long life and capacity to recreate itself were known prior to Christian times. Goodness knows how, because I find it hard to believe that your average Neolithic housewife might say with confidence to her new neighbour: 'Oh, yes, that tree's been here for more than 2,000 years.' Anyway, they knew, and hence the site of a yew tree often had spiritual associations that early Christians latched on to by building their places of worship next to such specimens.

The oak is the king of the forest, and English examples are superb, not least at Westonbirt. The wood is incredibly dense and strong, so beetles or worms cannot damage it. The trees are not affected by drought or extreme temperatures, they just keep on steadily growing. You get a tight molecular structure that is hard to cut, fashion or snap; hence its role in building wooden ships. And, of course, it makes wonderful furniture, particularly over time, as a patina or skin develops from polish and dirt, dirt and polish.

How long ago did man first work with wood? We can't be sure, but I can be certain that someone had invented or copied the wheel 3,000 years ago, because I have seen the evidence, thanks to Francis Pryor, an archaeologist who discovered a Bronze Age settlement in the Fens and delicately dug up the site. Among the wonderful artefacts unearthed were the segments of a wooden wheel patently designed to mobilise a cart of some sort. The body of the circle is made from planks of alder, resistant to rot and abrasion, and it has dovetailed cross-pieces cut from oak to hold these together; each section is pegged to the next by ash, which will absorb shocks and won't split. A pretty sophisticated item, patently the work of a knowledgeable wheelwright.

Man has also milled flour for a very long time. Once wheels could be constructed, a vital application would have been the turning of paddles to harness water power in a stream or river. Cogglesford Mill at Sleaford, south of Lincoln, produces flour in a traditional way, and it was a great pleasure to see the constituent parts of a very clever construction that allows a drive shaft to

The finished product.

turn. This has a cogged wheel at the top to gear it to a second wheel, providing a pulley system to lift sacks of flour between floors within the building, and ultimately to turn the circular stone that crushes and breaks up the corn.

As you know, I'm a tree hugger. Hence I'm of the view that every tree, alive or felled, is a precious thing. Let's treasure them – goodness knows, we need more.

Trees that have been felled should be used judiciously. One man who knows this is Bill Cook of Marlborough, a master wood-carver who runs a family restoration business with his sons. He has the biggest collection of antique woods for restoration that I know of. Bill Cook's workshops are in the Savernake Forest, where he stores wood and veneers that date back to the seventeenth century. The building is deliberately kept very damp, because veneers that dry will split and shrink. Bill's son Richard undertakes most of the intricate work of replacing a section of missing veneer from a piece of antique furniture. From the store he tracks down something of the right age, colour and grain, then cuts it to size in all three dimensions. Getting the visible angles right is relatively straightforward, as he can work off a template created from the gap in the furniture. But the depth is critical. The piece of veneer must fit perfectly into the hole and sit flat after glue has been applied and has dried. The underside of the veneer is shaved delicately until Richard is confident he will end up with an invisible mend.

At Tatton Park in Cheshire the groundsmen take pride in managing their diverse stock of trees. When one has to come down, they are deeply concerned that it is used to best advantage. A few years ago it was necessary for a 170-year-old oak to be felled (because it was suffering from dieback), and they were delighted that a pair of local craftsmen offered a novel and impressive means of utilising the timber. Garry Olsen and Peter Toaig decided to invite designers to bid for sections of the tree in

Working with Wood

order to make some attractive end-product from their portion. In all, seventy-five talented and determined people took away some part of the metre-diameter tree, from planks to bark, twigs to acorns, roots to sawdust. The results were wonderfully varied and imaginative. From that one oak came furniture, sculpture, tableware, picture frames, toys, games, dress patterns, bobbins and even paper. The results have been captured in a fascinating book entitled *One Tree*. It really does aid the appreciation of this wonderful and precious resource in our midst.

An example of Andrew Garlick's life work and dedication.

One of my favourite woodworkers is Andrew Garlick, the harpsichord-maker. How do you get started in such a specialised trade? Well, first you have to love and appreciate harpsichords. The pleasures of the instrument first touched Andrew as a child, when he heard one played in a National Trust property. Then as a teenager he met a girl whose mother had one. He married the girl (hopefully not just to get near her instrument) and could now have a little fiddle on her keys when the fancy took him. He decided he would like a harpsichord for himself. As an art student he couldn't afford to buy one, so he built one from scratch. How about that for a project!

He made it by following an old design he found in a library. He completed the task, but it didn't sound quite right, so he simply started again, until he got the hang of it. A bit like learning to ride a bike, but considerably more complicated. Now he's one of the world's experts in this sophisticated field and he makes harpsichords at the request of a few select international musicians. The bodies are constructed from lime, poplar and Swiss pine. And then he sticks in lots of clever metal twangy bits, of course. It takes two months to make a harpsichord from scratch, and they sell for up to £25,000.

Now that's what I call working with wood.

19

Pottering around the Lake District

You can keep Harry Potter, give me Beatrix any time. I loved her books as a child, and still do. If I thought I already had an affinity with her writing and the magnificent illustrations that accompany her glorious stories, imagine my added delight when, arriving at her cottage near Windermere, I discovered it looked and felt exactly as I had always believed the perfect country cottage should.

This is thanks, in part at least, to the National Trust, which has done a fantastic job is preserving and presenting the very best of a period property with appropriate contents.

It is chocolate-box, but it's no contrivance. This was how Beatrix lived. I had the huge pleasure of sitting where she sat and wrote, and looking out at the view, with in the foreground the

Paul Martin's Britain

vegetable patch where rabbits continue to burrow to this day (presumably on a National Trust retainer), while in the background we can see a charming stretch of lake and hill.

Our visit gave us one wonderful Insert film. The second one we planned was down on the water at the Steamboat Museum. We commissioned one of the boats to cross the lake, as I learned about the history of tourism in the area and the mechanics of these fine craft. When the steam launch was invented, it added instantly to the leisure potential of the Lake District. Wind power was far too unreliable to sustain regular and reliable sailings from the sides of the lake. Only when the steam launch came along could local entrepreneurs offer a consistent service.

The best bit of this Insert film was Blue at my side at the helm, enjoying the wind, water, waves and motion. The worst bit was Alan, the sound recordist, grumbling constantly. Cars, road drills and aircraft are a constant challenge to television sound recordists. They are required to deliver 'clean' sound to the edit suite; me or the guest talking clearly without any extraneous noises impacting on the dialogue. This allows the editor to cut in and out of the conversation at any point and so join together the best bits. That's impossible if one bit has me asking a question in a quiet field and the guest answering while a jet aircraft is flying overhead.

Pottering around the Lake District

There were no jets, cars or drills in the vicinity of the steam launch, but the chuff, chuff of the steam engine was an irritant in Alan's sensitive ears and expensive headphones. However, it was a noise that even he acknowledged he'd have to put up with. To minimise the acoustical problem he used his boom microphone – a big furry oval on the end of a light steel arm. This lifted his sound gathering away from the engine itself. We motored along and I began to ask my questions.

Things seemed fine, but suddenly Alan screamed. His fluffy microphone sheath was on fire. He had been holding it too near the hot top of the coal stove funnel and rising sparks had set it alight. He took immediate evasive action and thrust the mike down into the water to douse the flames. But unfortunately this ended with him leaning downward over the side of the vessel and his very up-market designer sunglasses dropped off the end of his nose and disappeared into the lake.

Taking the helm at the Steamboat Museum.

Had Beatrix Potter witnessed this farcical scene, I'm sure she could have woven it into a delightful tale about a bunny on a boat losing some special possession and hoping a water vole might come to the rescue. Our sound recordist knew no friendly water voles and so sulked for the rest of the afternoon, while Ian Young, the cameraman, and I just fell about laughing. Poor Al! It seemed his whole world had come to an end.

20

Wales, my Spiritual Home

Before *Flog It!* came along I spent about two days a week over a period of seven years driving all over the beautiful country of Wales. I had and felt a real connection with it. It must be the Cornishman in me, a fellow Celt! And what a good hunting ground it proved to be, not just for primitive Welsh furniture but for capturing stunning landscapes and meeting some wonderful people.

It was hard work at first, but over the years it proved rewarding, as I made countless trips right up north to Anglesea, stopping at Roger Jones's auction room in Colwyn Bay and Antony Parry's saleroom in Mold. Antony has become a good friend and an offscreen expert on *Flog It!* He still gives me the nod when something good comes up in his rooms.

Paul Martin's Britain

I would break the trip up around Machynlleth and call in on Sam Parry's shop, Richmond Antiques. This guy became my mentor and taught me what to look for. He opened up my eyes, and he certainly has some contacts. For a start, it helps to speak fluent Welsh and to know all the members of every WI in a 50-mile radius.

This was how I found some good honest places to buy period Welsh furniture, so of course, when I started to film with *Flog It!*, I wanted to go to Wales, and, as far as I was concerned, the more times the merrier.

I had a very bad throat on the day I was due to record our Charles Frederick Tunnicliffe Insert on the island of Anglesey.

Tunnicliffe was a celebrated wildlife artist who spent the second half of his life on Wales's Holy Island. For our Insert I was due to go to the charming village of Malltraeth, which sits at the head of the inlet above Malltraeth Bay in the south-west corner of the island. It was the middle of winter, there was snow on the ground and I had a shocking cold. Frankly, I wasn't in best form.

But looking at the originals of the great artist's work, and recalling some of his delightful illustrations for *Tarka the Otter* that I had enjoyed as a child, really lifted my spirits.

The previous day, at our valuation event at the Anglesey ferry port of Holyhead, I had quizzed our experts about what they hoped to see among the hundreds of objects being brought in for their attention. As *Flog It!* fans will know, sometimes those expectations are realised, and on other occasions no examples of the significant local artefact or art turn up.

We were based in the lovely Ucheldre Arts Centre – a converted convent chapel that lies well away from the harbour-side. It has terrific art exhibitions, concerts and events, plus a great bookshop and café.

Adam Partridge was aware of Tunnicliffe's local connections and I saw his face light up when halfway through the morning he

Wales, my Spiritual Home

The now two-tier Robert Stephenson bridge over the Menai Straits to Anglesey.

told me he'd found a man with a copy of *Shorelands Summer Diary*, the 1952 record of the painter's work, a delightful combination of vignetted scraper boards and water colours. Our contributor had acquired this along with half-a-dozen other books in a Llandudno auction. He had paid £3 for the books. Adam estimated the copy of the *Diary* should fetch at least £50.

Charles Tunnicliffe had grown up on his parents' farm in Cheshire, so had plenty of opportunities to observe domesticated animals and wildlife. The original 1928 edition of Henry Williamson's *Tarka the Otter* did not have any illustrations, and it was Charles's wife, Winifred, who persuaded her husband to submit some illustrations to the publisher to be included in a second edition. The notion was well received and it was decided to use wood engravings, which Charles produced. This commenced a fruitful vein of work for Charles, who went on to illustrate over a hundred books in the next decade.

Enchanted with the bird population of Anglesey, the Tunnicliffes moved to the charming village of Malltraeth. He stayed at Shorelands, a pretty bungalow overlooking the estuary from 1947 until his death in 1979. Upon his arrival Charles had begun a dedicated process of capturing exquisite images of every bird species that occupied or visited the island. This culminated in *Shorelands Summer Diary*. The celebrated bird illustrator Sir Peter Scott considered Tunnicliffe was the best. Praise indeed.

The success of this book established a strong relationship between Tunnicliffe and the Royal Society for the Protection of Birds. Tunnicliffe provided many iconic images used by the RSPB in the 1950s and 1960s. These included guillemots, razorbills, fulmars, kittiwakes and puffins, all in abundance on the South Stack sanctuary west of Holyhead.

Far too much talking at the Holyhead valuation event had left me with a very sore throat as I prepared to talk about Tunnicliffe at Shorelands with John Smith, the curator of the collection at the Oriel Gallery, Llangefni, where there is a permanent exhibition of his work. It was a freezing cold, miserable morning, I was shivering, and my voice was rasping. But I had a solution, which I will share with you.

Wales, my Spiritual Home

Get a banana, nibble a tiny piece off the end, and chew it gently. The oil in the fruit lubricates your mouth and throat. Fold what remains of the banana skin across the eaten end of the fruit and put it in your pocket or bag. Half an hour later, do the same thing again.

This will allow you to talk without croaking.

I survived the morning, and felt much better a couple of weeks later when we watched the *Diary* go for £80 at Mold, allowing the lucky man who had picked it up for £3 to pay his car tax at a stroke.

C.F. Tunnicliffe, *Geese and Hoar Frost*.

21

A Trip to Northern Ireland

I had no idea what to expect when we took *Flog It!* to Northern Ireland. I hadn't been there before, and was charmed by the people and the places we managed to see across just a few days.

We recorded a pair of programmes in Derry and another two in Belfast. I managed a fleeting visit to the Giant's Causeway, and longer introductions to the Belleek factory, the Ulster Museum art gallery, the Ulster Folk and Transport Museum and Gallery Antiques of Bangor, where Phyllis Arnold explained to me the history of silhouettes and then cleverly captured me in that form.

Our valuation venue was the magnificent Millennium Forum in Derry, a stylish new arts and community space reflecting a healthy renaissance within this charming old town.

The mass marketing of goods around Ireland became possible as a result of the spread of the railway network. Commercial travellers from Belfast would turn up on the train and have their samples transferred to a horse and cart for inspection at the local shops. At the Foyle Valley Railway Centre there is an engaging celebration of that vital railway age.

From Derry I headed south-west towards Donegal Bay to the village of Belleek, where the distinctive and popular ceramics come from. Production started here in the 1860s, when local farmer John Bloomfield decided to exploit the felspar in the local stone to make pots. His business swiftly expanded and needed dozens of experienced potters from Stoke-on-Trent. Currently 200 people work in the factory, some the direct descendants of the Staffordshire pioneers. The most remarkable Belleek pieces feature immensely delicate basketwork. There are two trade secrets to successfully manipulating the fine, unfired strands. First, the clay is mixed with gum Arabic, and secondly the potters wipe their fingers with olive oil.

I met a Belleek collector, Tony Herty, who told me about acquiring an almost complete dinner service from a woman in Fermanagh. Everything was there apart from one soup bowl. He wondered if this piece had been lost or broken, but, no, it served as the cat's water bowl, and she had no intention of parting with it.

Most of the firm's output these days is exported to the USA, Canada and Australia, where there are plenty of collectors.

Another memorable strand of vibrant art history from Northern Ireland has been linen production. This centred on Lisburn. Medieval Irish linen made from flax was extremely rough and basic. Locals described it as 'coorse as pratey oaten'. I'm not exactly sure what that means, but somehow it does convey the general idea. You can imagine yokels tilling the fields wearing itchy smocks made from the stuff.

Cutting a dash: Phyllis Arnold captured me in silhouette.

It was the controversial William of Orange who decided to develop higher-quality material that would have commercial value overseas. He shipped in talented cloth-makers from Holland, and looms and spinning-wheels were set up in cottages next to flax fields. Women would do the spinning and men the weaving.

Paul Martin's Britain

A distinctive aspect of the production process was laying the linen cloth out on fields to allow it to bleach in the sun. The weaver would then take his length of cloth to market and sell it alongside the animals and vegetables. Later, dedicated Linen Halls were established for the trade.

In the nineteenth century production was mechanised and moved into big factories in Lisburn and later Belfast. These were still busy until halfway through the twentieth century, though not entirely dedicated to pretty table decoration and quality garments. During the Second World War they turned out more than two million linen parachutes. There's a steady collector interest in everything from doilies to damask. I saw many fine examples, but, as they are not the easiest items to display, their appeal is limited.

Belfast was made a city in 1888 and, to reflect its new status, the White Linen Hall was knocked down and a City Hall was built on the site. This was completed in 1906 and still occupies a vital central role and it's where we held our valuation event.

The city's major thoroughfares and buildings are well proportioned and pleasing to view. The skyline is fast changing. New developments are growing apace, particularly around the docks, with the Waterfront Hall a powerful new presence that looks across Laganside to the Port of Belfast. There can be seen the pair of massive yellow cranes defining the site of the Harland and Wolff shipyard, once the largest in the world. The cranes appeared in the 1960s, a hundred years after Yorkshireman Edward Harland established a partnership with German marine draughtsman Gustav Wolff. Hundreds of ships emerged from these yards, not least in the Second World War, when 139 naval vessels were launched, including 6 aircraft-carriers and 47 corvettes. This was in spite of many severe German bombing raids, particularly in the spring of 1941, one night of which saw the deaths of over 700 people during air raids on the city.

Opposite: The *Titanic* memorial outside Belfast's City Hall.

The *Titanic* was launched from the Harland and Wolff yard in 1911, and, of course, no one could have predicted then how powerful a place that magnificent vessel's name would come to have in memorabilia circles. The City Council produces a neat *Titanic* Trail fold-up map for those wanting to explore the emotive subject.

Following the maritime tragedy, a sombre memorial was commissioned for the city featuring a representation of Thane standing over a drowned seaman, who is held up by two sea nymphs. The inscription reads: 'Erected to the imperishable memory of those gallant Belfast men whose names are here inscribed and who lost their lives on the 15th April 1912 by the foundering of the Belfast-built R.M.S. *Titanic* through collision with an iceberg on her maiden voyage from Southampton to New York.' Curiously, the names are not inscribed alphabetically. We may only wonder at the relative status of these people. Why is William Parr near the top and Albert Ervine at the bottom?

Imagine the dismay across the city as news of this disaster at sea spread. Many must have been anguished at the thought that some engineering factor might have had a bearing on the great ship's misfortunes. But work at the yard had to continue. The *Britannic* was the third of the White Star super-liners due to emerge from the Harland and Wolff yard. As she took shape, the First World War commenced and the Admiralty commanded that she be assigned as a hospital ship. She was launched in 1915. She was 275 metres in length and weighed 48,158 tons. (As a comparison, HMS *Belfast*, moored in the Thames by Tower Bridge, is a mere 187 metres and just 15,000 tons.) The *Britannic* served in the Mediterranean until she hit a German mine in 1916, which destroyed her.

As we have said on *Flog It!* on more than one occasion, beware of alleged *Titanic* artefacts, as the chances are they will be fakes. For a cross-section of real *Titanic* stuff, make your way to

Robinson's Saloon on Great Victoria Street, one of the best bars I've ever been in.

The Irish landscape is absolutely magnificent. Explore it at your leisure, and then see how leading artists have captured it in the spacious galleries of the museum that sits in the grounds of Belfast's Botanic Gardens.

Unquestionably the most powerful legacy of Irishness is the number of American Presidents whose parentage can be traced to the island. Remnants of the roots of Andrew Jackson, Ulysses Grant, Woodrow Wilson and a dozen more occupiers of Washington's White House are cunningly preserved and displayed to ensure a rich vein of tourism that will for ever do great business. A third of all US Presidents have ancestry traceable to Ulster.

Contemporary tourist guides and potted histories are at pains to tread delicately and diplomatically when it comes to aspects of the island's troubled past and tribal allegiances, but I discovered a book by Richard Hayward published in the 1930s with a title that has the potential to irritate some: *In Praise of Ulster*. It enthuses over the legacy of Protestant and Catholic alike and celebrates the Ulster dialect ('this hard, staccato, vital speech'), pointing out that it is a 'veritable storehouse of the English that was spoken at the courts of Elizabeth and James and Mary Queen of Scots', with a Shakespearian richness and colour that have been entirely lost in England.

I was certainly delighted at the language I encountered, phrases and terminology so distinctive and endearing. The place is an under-appreciated treasure. Go get some.

22

One Man, One City, One Mighty Scotland

The greatest Glaswegian? Kenny Dalgleash? Well the city does share two great football sides. Must be Billy Colony? It's a city full of sharp wit and humour! No – it's got to be Charles Rennie Macintosh. It seems to me, wherever you go in Glasgow, whether it is a building on the street, the street itself or just a small piece of architectural detail, there's always a lasting reminder; a testament to the man's genius.

We've been all over Scotland in the last six years, filming a fishing museum in Aberdeen, visiting the 42nd Black Watch in Perth, searching for the Loch Ness monster in Inverness, reading the *Beano* and the *Dandy* in Dundee, exploring Medical Science in Edinburgh and the list goes on. But still we keep coming back to Glasgow. Maybe it's because we all love Anita Manning and

Paul Martin's Britain

The exterior of the Glasgow School of Art, illustrating Mackintosh's organic style of architecture.

her high-rise saleroom in the heart of this electricity. But it was filming at the House of an Art Lover in Bellahouston Park, and at the Glasgow School of Art building, both designed by Mackintosh, that was most inspiring.

Charles Macintosh took to drawing at a young age, walking in the hills to sketch the landscape, as well as the buildings of his native Glasgow. His sketchbooks are evidence of a budding talent, a fascination with form, both natural and man-made. At the age of 15 he was accepted as a student at the Glasgow School of Art, and the next year he was articled to a small local architect's firm, and combined his studies with earning a living over the next few years. It was at the school that he met a like-minded visionary student, Herbert Macnair, 'Bertie'.

At college they met Margaret Macdonald and Frances Macdonald, not sisters, but both young women with an appetite for fresh design and stylist fun; Charles was to marry Margaret in 1890, and Bertie married Frances in 1899. Also in 1890 Charles undertook his first substantial piece of commercial work: a house for his uncle. This was followed by designs for a rural villa, an arts club, a medical college and some tea rooms.

Charles was familiar with the work and values of William Morris and Dr Christopher Dresser, and they heavily influenced his work. He was also inspired by Venetian architecture after a trip to Venice and was deeply moved by the quality of architecture and the Italian capacity to integrate internal design and furnishing with appropriate frontage.

Swiftly and incisively, Charles Rennie Macintosh drove forward a style of design that was distinctive and memorable. He was aware of the movements around him, and the influences of William Morris, the Arts and Crafts movement and Audrey Beardsley are visible in the shapes and structures he pursued. He also drew on aspects of Japanese form and representation.

In the height of his career he won the commission to design a new home for the Glasgow School of Art and with this he applied all his perceptions, style, understanding and instincts. It became and remains a classic and glorious tribute to the man.

23

Fabulous Furniture

I could go on, and on, and on . . . and on about favourite pieces of furniture. And one day I will (publishers, please note). But this is not the place to do so, so I have confined myself to a few examples that you can see for yourselves and thus appreciate what stimulates my enthusiasm for the subject.

I have been lucky enough to gain access to some private collections and individual pieces that are enjoying pride of place in someone's home. But this book is about what we can democratically share and enjoy, so I've picked out just a few bits of brown furniture that can be viewed by anyone who gets on a bus or train and can pay, if necessary, an entrance fee to enter the premises.

In historical order, let me begin with a wonderful vernacular seventeenth-century oak table that is just down the road from me at Lacock Abbey. In a lovely big sitting room, National Trust staff sit at this table, checking passes and taking entrance fees. It has a marvellous patina, and shows some admirable wear. Because the wood is so old, it has a tighter grain and so holds polish better. Its strength for me is the fact that it is an appreciated antique with a

I was enchanted by this English walnut double dome bureau bookcase of 1710 from the Noel Terry collection at Fairfax House.

contemporary function. I envy the family who currently occupy the house. I would love to have a supper party at this table – a dozen friends sitting around enjoying wine, pasta and good bread off this 300-year-old piece of working furniture.

When my mum comes to stay, I often take her into the Abbey, which houses an eclectic mix of furniture, with representative pieces from various ages – a principle that I greatly appreciate, and aspire to achieve for myself over time.

Probably the most significant item is a tilting tea table designed by Thomas Chippendale. That doesn't mean he personally laid a finger on it, or even that he ever saw it, because what this Yorkshireman did in 1754 was publish a book of designs, *The Gentleman and Cabinet Maker's Director* – a sort of pioneering DIY guide to fine furniture making. The sets of drawings were greatly appreciated, and many cabinet-makers around the country slavishly followed the forms Chippendale had either created or recommended; hence the description 'Chippendale chair' normally indicates a design, rather than a woodworker. The Lacock example is an early eighteenth-century walnut piece with a birdcage mechanism at the top of the central column, which allowed the table to be revolved – so you could reach your tea.

The Abbey dates back to the thirteenth century, when it was founded by Ela, Countess of Salisbury, in memory of her late husband, William Longespee. He had a number of claims to fame, including witnessing the signing of Magna Carta and laying the foundation stones of Salisbury Cathedral, which wasn't bad for the bastard son of Henry II.

In York's city centre is perhaps one of the finest examples of eighteenth-century architecture, Fairfax House, designed by John Carr. Sadly in recent years the city council has seen fit to surround it with an urban concrete jungle to its rear elevation, obstructing a view from its impressive windows. But it is in fact what is inside that attracts me.

Restored to its former glory in the 1980s by York Civic Trust, Fairfax House contains possibly the finest collection of Georgian furniture in the world. This was collected by the late Noel Terry, the man behind the 'chocolate orange', who had a lot of money and a passion for fine furniture. To see Fairfax House is to see Georgian splendour and a dictionary of English furniture in its true surroundings.

Burghley House near Stamford was the country seat of William Cecil, confidant of Elizabeth I. No expense was spared in shaping the exterior, and furnishing the huge complement of grand rooms. Then along came the English Civil War and a troop of soldiers was garrisoned there. How did these uncouth, uncaring brutes ride out the cold winter? By burning all the furniture. When royalty got back in the saddle, the 5th Earl of Essex was seriously short of seats. And, cruelly adding injury to insult, the Great Fire of London had coincidentally destroyed the workshops of most of the best English furniture-makers. There was only one answer: the earl would have to head off to mainland Europe and buy up some stuff to fill his cavernous headquarters.

One early port of call was Pierre Gole's premises outside Paris. Here his lordship managed to pick up a brand new cabinet on a stand. It was a Louis XIV-style piece rich in exotic softwood marquetry, providing exquisite decoration and detail ranging in colour from black ebony to off-white satin wood. It's still in the house now – a gloriously elaborate piece that fits perfectly with the whole excess and grandeur of Burghley.

Now let's move forward 150 years and consider a desk that has a well-defined place in history. It was made in 1815 by George Bullock in London. That was the year of the Battle of Waterloo, when Napoleon Bonaparte was defeated and exiled to the Isle of St Helena. When the deposed dictator got there, he decided to write his memoirs, and of course needed a decent desk for the job, which is where the Bullock piece came in. The War Office in London ordered it and shipped it over to the sulking ex-emperor, and he used it daily as he scribbled notes on what went wrong and why, until he died in 1821. Six years later the 2nd Earl of Carnarvon managed to buy it off the cleric who had been Napoleon's personal chaplain.

This fine mahogany desk with cabriole legs and claw feet now sits in the library at Highclere Castle. This had been a relatively modest house on an estate just south of Newbury in Berkshire until the 3rd Earl had it expanded and redesigned by Charles Barry in the manner of his celebrated Palace of Westminster.

We undertook a valuation day in the castle's saloon, whose walls are covered in tooled Spanish leather. Mercifully it was a fine, dry day, as I dread to think of the damage that could have been done to those walls by soaking anoraks brushing past.

The extensive library was put together by the 4th Earl, who was one of Disraeli's cabinet ministers. The 5th Earl dug up Tutankhamun in Egypt and dropped dead soon afterwards, which some people reckoned was the mummies getting their own back. Under the 8th Earl's management, wedding ceremonies are held in the castle, but they don't come cheap. Jordan the voluptuous model and her beau Peter André got hitched here. Perhaps they signed their names on the very desk that Napoleon had hunched over nearly two centuries earlier. There's a bust of Napoleon in the library, but no bust of Jordan, perhaps because it might topple off the shelf.

A journey to Cheltenham (oh, hardship) takes us towards the twentieth century. In this exquisite town's Art Gallery and Museum we can relish – for free – a fantastic collection of Arts and Crafts furniture. There are pieces made by William Morris and a glorious cross-section of Arts and Crafts work from the multiplicity of workshops and studios that were dotted about the Cotswolds from the 1870s until the 1940s.

Paul Martin's Britain

You need to devote at least half a day to wandering through the Cheltenham Arts and Crafts collection, which includes an early circular Morris table with strong, confident, fundamental lines; powerful and distinctive. The job of this chapter is to alert you to a few of my favourites. At Cheltenham it's agony to have to make a choice, but it is this: a sideboard designed by Charles Voysey for some exacting but appreciative clients, Mr and Mrs Ward Higgs. This couple had the capacity, resources and taste to commission a range of work from Voysey, some of the best of which has now been gathered here for all to enjoy.

Oak sideboard by Sidney Barnsley, 1924.

Sidney and Ernest Barnsley were two brothers who literally followed Morris, by moving from London to the Cotswolds, where they built their own houses at Sapperton using local materials and traditional techniques. Then they got stuck into distinctive furniture making, deploying whole planks of wood as their starting point for each piece, and celebrating the construction techniques by exposing their neatly executed joints. Sidney's son, Edward, was born in 1900 and grew up in this creative atmosphere, playing among the wood and chippings. Edward went off to a progressive school in Petersfield in Hampshire, and then trained at a workshop nearby. In a few years he took over the business, and began to employ more craftsmen who had the skills and interest to pursue the Barnsley style, a combination of his father's Arts and Crafts form with the addition of elegant curves, fine inlays and exotic woods.

Edward died in 1987, but the workshop continues to produce marvellous furniture and in parallel provides training for talented craftsmen who want to make a piece of furniture all by themselves that doesn't look as though it's come out of a catalogue or an evening class. The centre is run by James Ryan, who gave me a guided tour and showed me an example of Sidney's work, an oak dresser from 1898 that exposes the jointing cut by hand, and features metalwork forged by a blacksmith specifically for the piece. This contrasts with a walnut bureau made by Edward in 1977 as a commission for Lord Brierley for the Queen's Silver Jubilee exhibition. It cost £4,000 at the time and is now worth £35,000. Yes, the problem that caused Morris anguish still remains. Individually designed, hand-made furniture cannot come cheap. The business needs wealthy clients.

But I still say: why do so many people head for IKEA when they can acquire something distinctive and hand-crafted in solid wood from a decent auction?

24

Great Gardening

I'm not a great gardener, but I know a man who is. And plenty of women, too. I am a great garden appreciator. And I do hereby assure Charlotte that the moment I stop presenting television programmes six days a week, I will do more on our demanding patch.

The wonderful thing about gardens is that we can all make them and all appreciate them. And most of us do. Whether you have a window box or run to a hundred acres, you can plan, plant, nurture, study and treasure the development of dozens of different botanical species. They are never the same two days running, which, of course, is both the pleasure and the problem of gardens. They are constantly evolving, sometimes coming close to how you would ideally wish them to look, sometimes frustratingly far away.

Let's explore some of my favourite gardens. Unfortunately it must be pointed out that few of these places are easy to reach by public transport. Unlike most of the sites mentioned in this book, the majority in this chapter are somewhat challenging to get to without a car.

I'm pleased to say there are dedicated bus services from several towns in Cornwall to the Eden Project, so we'll begin there.

You've got a great big hole in the side of a hill. What do you do with it? Offer it to the council as a new landfill site, or turn it into an environmentally friendly park? You voted for the latter? Good decision. Tim Smit played round with this notion for a very long time before he started to acquire a critical mass of support that meant dreams could be turned into reality.

Tim was a semi-retired record producer who dug up the Lost Gardens of Heligan, and then engaged and negotiated with the great and the good of Cornwall and beyond to nurture in the minds of the Millennium Commission the idea that a collection of giant 'biomes' should be one of the dozen Landmark Projects. He successfully built up an irresistible head of steam and

Croome Park in
Worcestershire.

eventually steered the delivery of this extraordinary educational and celebratory centre. If you're interested in understanding the inspiration that brought about such a high-profile end result, read Tim's book *Eden*, where he points out that the undertaking was designed to 'inspire people to reflect on the vital role of plants and come to understand the need for a balance between husbandry – growing them for our use, and stewardship – taking care of them on behalf of all living things'.

Now to the National Botanic Garden of Wales, north of Swansea. Again it is not easy to reach by public transport, but it can be done – by bus from Carmarthen Railway Station. This site had been occupied by one of the most handsome mansions in the principality until 1931, when William Paxton's palace burnt down. Paxton had made his money as Master of the Mint in Bengal in the late eighteenth century, and he decided to retire to south Wales and here commission a fine house surrounded by extraordinary water gardens engineered with complicated systems of plumbing to allow water to cascade between features.

In the 1980s a local artist, William Wilkins, rediscovered the remnants of the original sophisticated gardens, and this propagated the seeds of a formidable round of proposals, planning and perseverance that grew into the fine complex opened by the Prince of Wales in July 2000. It is spacious and stylish and provides handsome pathways and sculpted features with gracious and unique collections of wonderful plants, many, naturally, in their infancy. I think it's somewhere of which you should get a snapshot now and then revisit in twenty years to see how richly textured it will have become thanks to Mother Nature and good professional gardening.

They rightly give a special place to Welshman Alfred Russel Wallace, who, in the 1850s, developed the notion of the origin of the species completely independently of Charles Darwin, and possibly before the Englishman had committed himself to the massively significant notion. Alas, Wallace remained in the publicity undergrowth, just not in the right place at the right time.

Before science and technology were brought to bear on botany, the appearance of decorative parkland was entirely dependent on hard work, a good eye and endless amounts of money. The noble Temple family hurled mountains of the stuff at their Stowe estate, commissioning grand interiors to be matched by magnificent landscaping. Lancelot Brown was promoted to the job of head gardener here in 1741. Nice number, you might think, but this boy was looking for broader horizons. Maybe he got fed up with the boss's demands for temples to be erected across the grounds (those Temples liked temples), but he went freelance. His first stop as an independent was Croome Park in Worcestershire, where the Earls of Coventry put up their feet. The 6th Earl had inherited an enormous stretch of bogland, and decided to turn it into something more appealing. Brown was signed up to tackle the task and soon was shaping an ornamental lake and river between pleasing hillocks, with a little help from hundreds of men with spades and wheelbarrows.

The results were well received by the well heeled and so Brown became a hot property. Lots of aristocrats wanted his input. From his headquarters in Hammersmith he would head off and assess their estates and often describe what he saw as having 'capabilities'. Hence he acquired the nickname Capability Brown.

The National Trust has put in huge efforts to restore Croome Park to its original glory, replanting 45,000 trees and shrubs and removing 50,000 cubic metres of silt from the river and lake. It's well worth a visit, though not easy to reach by public transport. A taxi from Pershore railway station might be the best option.

If you are in Northern Ireland, be sure to explore the Botanic Gardens in Belfast – a couple of modest but absorbing hot houses, one of which is a beautiful and atmospheric 1840s pioneering cast-iron and glass structure created by the Dublin architect Richard

Turner, who went on to engineer and construct the great Palm House at Kew.

Next, hop over to Harrogate, where a brisk walk from the railway station will eventually take you to Harlow Carr. The local spring water encouraged Henry Wright to establish a spa facility here in 1844, complete with ornamental gardens. That was four years before the railway arrived in town. The accessibility of the spa hugely advanced Harrogate's social standing, and the town's elegance has enhanced its status across Yorkshire and beyond to this day. The gardens suffered through the two world wars, but in 1946 the Northern Horticultural Society chose the site to test plants for their hardiness, and so the place started to flourish once more. Now it has become the fourth and most northerly of the Royal Horticultural Society's gardens and is thus enjoying blossoming prospects.

'Tea for 2', or was that 'Tea for 200'? Recycling at Harlow Carr.

Coming down the right-hand side of England, just above Rutland Water we arrive at a great garden that many of you will have already seen, because in various forms, at various times, it has appeared in hundreds of television programmes. The Budget Garden, the Living Garden, the Ornamental Kitchen Garden, the Artisan's Cottage Garden. Who created them? A London boy who took a horticulture diploma in Essex, then set up a commercial garden centre in Northamptonshire and started writing for *Gardening News*.

He soon got to present a gardening series for Anglia Television, and then became editor of *Practical Gardening*. Next step up the ladder was a short feature for *Gardener's World*. This went down so well that he soon became a regular, then found some fields and started to create gardens from scratch, much to the joy of the television producers and their growing audiences.

The Stoney Road allotments.

Yes, it was Geoff Hamilton, the star of television gardening through the 1980s. And here's a big secret. For several of those television series, Geoff first built a new garden at Barnsdale Gardens, then, a year later, started to create a replica in front of the cameras. This allowed him to proceed with confidence, knowing his end results would be satisfactory. And it meant the producers could point cameras at the finished, flourishing beds on the very same day as they filmed Geoff digging the holes.

Let's get down to earth now and take the train to Coventry. Alongside the railway line is a delightful, egalitarian complex of gardens – the Stoney Road allotments. This is not simply a series of utilitarian vegetable patches, but exquisitely distinctive individual gardens, each one of which would seem to demand a house to go with it.

And the charming thing is some of them do have their own houses – tiny, cute brick buildings, which look like Hansel and Gretel cottages, inside which you can keep your tools and light a fire and brew up some tea – which is how they have been used since they were set up for ex-soldiers following the Napoleonic Wars. Every one is a little gem.

Those women I mentioned? Well, Gertrude Jekyll would be at the top of my list. She designed around 400 gardens between the 1890s and 1920s, few of them, alas, still in the form in which she created them. One fascinating example is the garden at Upton Grey Manor in Hampshire. This was the home of Charles Holme, editor of *The Studio*, the influential Arts and Crafts magazine.

Holme, whose money had come from his family's fabric business, commissioned Jekyll to produce a fitting plan for his 4-acre site in 1908.

She was aged 65 at this time, full of energy and ideas. It took several years to construct and bed in the elements, and she considered the results one of her most satisfactory achievements. Of course gardens don't stay beautiful unless you put plenty of work into them. And with moves, changes of ownership and deaths, the Upton Grey garden of Gertrude Jekyll was completely overgrown and abandoned by the end of the Second World War. Then along came Rosamund Wallinger, who purchased the semi-derelict property with her husband in 1984. They had no idea that the bramble- and weed-dense grounds had any significance. But when they learned of the Jekyll roots, they decided to try to restore the garden to the form and glory it had once boasted. They researched Gertrude's documents held in a Californian archive, and ordered replacement plants for the ones that had long gone. Elements of the existing foliage were given serious attention with pruning-hooks, and loving care was applied to walls and pathways. The work is not yet complete, but it's proceeding well, a huge tribute to Jekyll and to the Wallingers. Enjoy some views at www.gertrudejekyllgarden.co.uk.

Upton Grey Manor: the restored gardens in full bloom.

Now it would be idiotic of me to start to make suggestions about what you might plant in your garden. But I could make a few proposals about where you could go to seek objects to complement your plants. I used to spend lots of time exploring depots handling salvaged garden ornaments, a vital element in my magazine photography design work. Perhaps the very best place to buy up old objects to enhance your plot is at the Talisman site in Dorset, and now in the New King's Road in London. My old mate Ken has sumptuous options available for those on a generous budget. The last time I was there the top of the range was a glorious configuration of marble carved and constructed in India in 1840. Asking price: £50,000.

Frankly it would look shamefully gnome-like next to Britain's biggest and most outrageous single item of garden decoration, which is at Witley Court in Worcestershire.

This was the elaborate home of the Earls of Dudley, who, thanks to fortunes made from Black Country mining and metal-bashing, were able to indulge in a fanciful house and matching over-the-top gardens. They were big on fountains and in 1854 called on the services of master garden designer and fountain builder William Nesfield to knock up a monster in their back yard. His *Perseus and Andromeda* was Europe's biggest fountain, a no-holds-barred confection of exotic creatures spurting water in all directions in the middle of a huge artificial pond. Not in a public square for the common benefit for the good people of Dudley, but as a private amusement for the family while they breakfasted on the terrace.

The house burnt down in 1937 and the remains were allowed to deteriorate. Local kids would run around the ruins at weekends, without any regard to safety or security. They explored underground service tunnels designed for plumbers to maintain the fountains. It was a wonderful adventure playground that no right-minded adult or health and safety inspector would condone.

The impressive fountain at Witley Court.

Then English Heritage took it over and immediately stuck barbed wire around the outskirts so it could no longer be a danger to innocent children. Now the fountain has been restored and it's a glorious sight, which every visitor can enjoy.

25

Beach Combing

You can't beat a good wander along a beach. It never fails to lift and enrich heart and soul. When my parents moved to Falmouth, I found the beach took my mind off what I felt I was missing from London. I became absorbed by the fall of the waves, the noise of the surf, the beckoning horizon and the fresh scatter of objects on the sand revealed by each receding tide.

When first in Falmouth I didn't know my tides. A city boy is aware they go in and out, but he doesn't appreciate the cyclical patterns and daily incremental changes. From high tide it takes around six hours for the water to reach a low point, then another six hours or so for it to come in again, the precise time interval altering day by day.

Paul Martin's Britain

It took a lot of wandering stretches of Cornish coast before I began to identify patterns and then have sailors explain to me how it all works. I was just pleased that it was ever changing. And each time the tide went out, things were washed up on the beach that hadn't been there before: shells, stones, seaweed, driftwood, plastic rubbish. When Robin Knox-Johnston first single-handedly traversed the oceans nearly forty years ago, he recorded that occasionally he could see bits of plastic bobbing on the water. Now ocean yachtsmen and women report that there is almost never a time when they look at the sea and fail to be aware of some indestructible flotsam or jetsam impinging on the beauty of nature. Where has all that plastic come from? Thrown overboard from ships? Floated out of river mouths? Chucked over cliff tops? Yes, all those ways. Shame on us for allowing our junk to get everywhere.

So I would wander the beaches and be drawn to the innocent charm of shells and stones and slivers of tree branch. One often comes across sections of sawn timber that have been soaked and weathered, but these pieces seem charmless compared with the length of unhandled wood that has fallen from a trunk in a storm and so entered the sea and been carried by currents for hundreds, maybe thousands, of miles. This has an exotic quality, an honest appeal.

Shells are different, however. Here we are dealing with the natural habitat of some deceased sea creature. The animal has passed away, and so its mobile home becomes even more mobile, as there is no longer a sticky foot attaching it to a stable rock. I have gathered up many a shell in my time, both at home and abroad. Nothing matches the dawn discovery of a fine example. Some people will buy shells from shops, which any self-respecting adult should find horribly pointless.

Question: how old is your average beach-discovered shell? Probably less than five years. However, on some beaches we may be able to track down shells that are five million years old. Yes, fossils.

Paul Martin's Britain

Below and opposite:
The Sutcliffe Gallery in
Whitby houses dozens of
great postcards of the
Victorian photographer's
work, here showing the
big business generated
by the local jet.

There are certain parts of our coastline where erosion is washing away particular types of rock that will expose ancient shells, or the impression of them, because time and pressure have turned the shell to stone. One of my favourite fossil spots is Lyme Regis in Dorset, where a few hours of diligent examination of the exposed rocks should lead you at least to a tiny example of an ammonite. Some of the North Yorkshire beaches may also yield a fossil. In theory this could be a dinosaur fragment, but is more likely to be a remnant of an 180-million-year-old monkey puzzle tree. That's where Whitby jet comes from. A dawn beach walk can disclose nuggets of black stuff, about the size of a walnut. Have some wet and dry sandpaper with you, and give the lump a rub. If a black mark is scored on to the paper, it means you've got a piece of coal in your hand. However, if the mark on the sandpaper is brown, then you could be looking at jet.

Carving and polishing jet in Victorian times was big business in Whitby. The stuff was perfect holiday souvenir material. Ironically, it got the royal seal of approval when Queen Victoria decided to wear fine examples of the cut and decorated mineral in brooches to mourn the death of her husband, Albert. There were 200 workshops chiselling and buffing jet at one time. Walrus hide was used to give smooth surfaces, and the piece would be finished with rouge powder spun against the little ornament on a lambswool wheel. This would spray red dust on to the

operator, who would then unintentionally scare children on his way home from work – one of the wild and weird Whitby red devils.

Heading southward we eventually get to Southwold, and lines of handsome, coloured beach huts, looking out on another treasure from the earth's past. Twice a week someone discovers an orange stone the size of a cherry that turns out to be amber. This is far younger than jet: a mere fifty million years old. It's the fossilised sap of pine trees. And, as we know from *Jurassic Park*, there's a sliver of a chance it may contain the remains of a tiny insect. Robin Fernell runs a shop and a museum of amber and showed me some of his most impressive items. The biggest raw piece of amber was about the size of a loaf of bread. This would be worth £5,000 uncut and unpolished. But beware of fake amber. How do you spot it? Stick a hot pin into the material. If the smell reminds you of pine, you're in business; if it stinks of plastic, you've been had.

26

Travelling through Time

*I*magine being able to take every edition of every map ever made of any part of the country and getting them all sized up to the same scale and then putting one on top of the other in chronological order from medieval times to the present day.

We would have a plot of the paths of the advance of the Industrial Revolution, and a sense of how our contemporary conurbations were born and when they grew. What it would tell us is that, until the time of Elizabeth I, our whole way of life hinged on the rivers. These provided transport, food and power, as well as barriers to travel. Bridges were rare and crucial. Commerce and power were concentrated in those places where people were forced to gather to get across a major river. This was where our villages and towns began to grow.

Stourport today is the base for plenty of narrow boats, used as full-time homes or holiday retreats.

River fish were a vital commodity, and landowners judiciously controlled access to their banks in order to manage the assets in the water. Mill-owners needed water to power their corn mills and their woollen mills. They wanted to guide the water into gullies that would feed power to the paddles. Meanwhile merchants wanted to move boats up and down stream, using horses or men to drag and push heavily laden vessels from inland town to sea port and back.

There was serious conflict over the use of rivers. Land transport was immensely difficult. Horses could traverse fields and negotiate woodland, but getting a cart or carriage from A to B was hugely troublesome. In the seventeenth century serious attempts were made to make the rivers reliably navigable. Locks were established, and steadily the movement of boats greatly improved. Trackways were established in order to make the riverside accessible by cart, and some were laid with rails to make the movement of those carts more smooth and manageable. And when the principle of pound locks – holding merely a canal-boat-sized rectangle of water – became established, the notion of building a waterway tangentially from the river took hold quite abruptly.

The aptly titled Duke of Bridgewater was out in front. He owned coal in Worsley, 9 miles north of Manchester. It was difficult and expensive to cart this fuel to the town, so Bridgewater decided to invest in a dedicated route that took the coal in boats above the River Irwell and straight to a quay, where it could be sold at a far lower price than the coal transported by road or river. That was in 1759. The canal age was born. Within a few years dozens of canal schemes were under way. No longer was traffic confined to natural waterways; canals could go anywhere within reason, if money and men were able to bridge valleys, hack tunnels and cut clay and rock.

Improved transport blossomed in parallel with increasing appetites for manufacture. Iron could be smelted into many useful forms. This needed huge amounts of coal, which could now be moved from mine to factory by boat. Large quantities of water were also essential for most manufacturing tasks, so workplaces grew around the rivers, canals, towns and mines.

Steam power was in its infancy. A steam engine could drive belts and so power machines. The next step was putting the steam engine on wheels so it could move itself. These engines were extraordinarily heavy and so needed rails to traverse the land, but by 1830 such a system had joined Liverpool

The *Mallard* at the National Railway Museum in York.

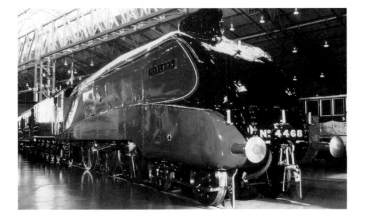

175

to Manchester. Within a lifetime, canals were about to be superseded. Railways had more power and greater speed. Rail mania now proceeded just as canal development had done, determined entrepreneurs seeing opportunities to join mine to factory, town to town, coast to coast.

The next stop was the internal combustion engine. Victoria was still on the throne when motor vehicles were starting to use the roads. One hundred years later there would be thirty million of them on British highways.

It's been my pleasure and privilege to visit many of the preserved structures of our Industrial Revolution. During the past fifty years lots of factories, mills and chimneys have become an embarrassing reminder of an earlier time, the ugly remnants of a harsh regime. And many were summarily demolished to make way for retail parks and housing estates.

However, towards the end of the twentieth century, planners and conservationists started to argue that Victorian mills were not a blot on the landscape, but proud monuments to our ancestors' ingenuity and hard work. Many have now been saved from destruction and instead given new life – as homes, hotels, museums, shops and arts centres.

While life for their original occupants was often rough, tough, frugal and sometimes horribly short, these great buildings from the industrial age may now be seen to have their own grace and charm. Track them down and appreciate them, but never forget the people who devoted their lives to working within them and hence sustaining those sturdy edifices. Every one of these vast buildings had dedicated

The rush hour in Bakewell.

chimneys churning out coal furnace smoke every day of the week. The atmosphere was thick with fug, not helped by the fact that everyone over the age of 9 smoked tobacco – yes, usually at about the same time as they first went to work. Towards the end of the nineteenth century Monet came from France to paint Big Ben on the Thames. His image shows a heavy, muggy mush over the river, barely broken up by a glimmer of red light. Was this a moody, impressionistic image, or an accurate portrayal of how little light and horizon a London smog permitted?

I hope the *Flog It!* programmes and this book acknowledge the debt we owe to the men and women who drove and delivered our wealth and the texture of our landscape.

Ironbridge Gorge, a testament to the genius of Thomas Telford.

27

Tracking Isambard

Brunel must have made thousands of journeys along parts of what we would now call the M4 corridor, determining, then executing, the route of the Great Western Railway.

What a job. Crossing farmers' fields to identify a viable course that minimised gradients, working out how to get through or around hills and valleys. Then commissioning the construction of the track and the erection of stations and all the other services that a brand new means of transport would require.

And he did it all with style and grace and smart solutions to engineering problems.

His father, Marc Brunel, was a French civil engineer who had won a series of commissions from the Royal Navy for dock facilities. Marc then went on to tackle a tunnel under the Thames, from Rotherhide to Wapping, but became overwhelmed by the difficulties of successfully cutting a hole under the city's river.

Isambard Kingdom worked for his dad for a while and then visited Bristol, where he learned of ambitions to bridge the Avon Gorge at Clifton. At the age of just 21 he submitted a design for the project – in competition with the grand old man of civil engineering, Thomas Telford – and eventually won.

Audaciously, IK now applied for the job of engineer to the proposed Great Western Railway and once again came out on top.

The young man faced a monumental task but demonstrated an extraordinary determination to overcome all obstacles with a rare combination of aesthetic appeal and pioneering mechanics. Imposing buildings, elegant bridges and stylish, dedicated ancillary services were the hallmark of the GWR. Remember, in those early days this wasn't a transport system for the likes of you and me. It was for the upper classes and their accompanying servants. Hence elegant stations, luxury carriages and lavish attention from liveried staff.

Standing in the wooden superstructure: a half-finished ash railway carriage, at the Great Western Railway Museum in Swindon.

One thing Brunel wasn't so good at was making locomotives. His first efforts could barely get up a head of steam. The railway company decided to buy their engines from Robert Stephenson – the other great railway engineer, son of George, the Geordie locomotive pioneer. So the early GWR engines were shipped down from Stephenson's factory in Newcastle upon Tyne.

Over time Isambard and Robert became friendly rivals, building Britain's infrastructure and their careers in parallel.

Fred Dibnah regularly enthused about both engineers, wonderfully communicating to me and millions of others the significance of their mastery and manipulation of metal and deployment of steam power to advance the Victorian agenda.

Brunel's legacy now enjoys greater public appreciation, though the Stephenson school is always ready to argue the case that their man technically has more to his name and statistically contributed to a greater range of engineering developments than the stove-hatted one. Ultimately, Brunel made a bigger aesthetic impact, and if we hop off the M4 at various points we can quickly access and appreciate a significant selection of his endeavours.

East to west, make first for Didcot Railway Centre, where you can examine a length of broad-gauge railway, and, joyously, see the kind of steam locomotive that first perambulated those confident tracks. At Didcot they have recreated a train – hauled by a replica *Fire Fly* locomotive – that matches Brunel's vision for the new mode of transport.

Broad gauge was abandoned in 1892. There's a poignant picture in Steven Brindle's fabulous book about Brunel showing a hundred or more locomotives lined up ready for scrap or converting when the change to Stephenson's recommended narrower gauge was universally applied.

Swindon was the halfway house of the original GWR track, and so the ideal place to develop engineering works, stores and services. This was done on an extraordinary scale. A whole new town was created to house the workers who were building every element that the railway required. At the start of the twentieth century 12,000 men were employed. The Works would close down for ten days each summer and every employee got a free rail ticket to the seaside and back, but received no holiday pay.

Alfred Williams wrote a sobering account of *Life in a Railway Factory* in 1915. He was an iron drop-stamper in a carriage shed and described the working environment of the steam hammers:

> There is no escape for the eye; nothing but bricks and mortar, iron and steel, smoke and steam arising. The men dexterously guide the spluttering and fizzing ingots with tongs. Sparks travel a great distance burning everything they meet. To protect themselves the men wear heavy iron jackboots, reaching above their knees, with an iron veil over their eyes and faces. Gradually the blows fall harder. The steam spouts, roars and hisses; the chains jingle and the ground under your feet shakes as though in an earthquake.

Head into Swindon's STEAM – Museum of the Great Western Railway – and relish its recreation of scenarios from the great Works, as well as some glorious locomotives, each with character and impact. You can see why the Revd Mr Awdry felt that individual engines had particular personalities, and how his books and subsequently the television version of Thomas the Tank Engine and his friends became such a hit. One can almost see a face on the front of each of the huge machines.

Moving on to Bristol, we find two of Brunel's most extraordinary achievements. First comes a flavour of the man's maritime endeavours. The SS *Great Britain* was the second of three audacious vessels he designed to cross the Atlantic. The aim was to connect London to New York via Bristol. The paddle-driven SS *Great Western* had commenced these services in 1838.

The iron-hulled, propeller-driven *Great Britain* made the same voyage in 1845, taking a mere fourteen days. The ship featured a great deal of complicated and pioneering marine engineering. It was the biggest vessel in the world when launched, too big for Bristol's docks. She was assigned to Liverpool but a year later ran aground off the Irish coast, where she stayed for a year before being repaired and refloated.

Brunel was by now working on the *Great Eastern* – an even bigger and bolder ship constructed on the Thames, but the fortunes of the Great Western Steamship Company sank rapidly and the fleet was sold off, the *Great Eastern* ending up cable-laying across the Atlantic – never what its designer had had in mind. The *Great Britain* was allocated to services to and from Australia, then assigned to store goods in the Falklands, where she subsequently sank. It is a huge credit to the many Brunel enthusiasts that she was refloated and brought back to England

A fabulous day out at the Museum of the Great Western Railway at Swindon.

Paul Martin's Britain

and returned to the dock where she has been built. Steven Brindle writes: 'She is arguably the single most important vessel, in terms of ship design, in history.'

Take a look at this wonder. The experience is enhanced by the excellent presentation, with a segment of Perspex creating a sea surface on which we can see ducks paddling close to the hull. Then we can climb down some steps and enjoy the same scene seemingly from underwater.

Brunel's other big triumph in Bristol is his suspension bridge at Clifton across the Avon Gorge. Its foundation stone was laid in 1831, but almost immediately social problems in and around the city inhibited progress. We're talking riots – citizens demanding representation in parliament and an end to the rotten boroughs. More than a hundred protestors were killed or wounded in three days of rioting in October that year. Business confidence was severely dented and by 1843 only the towers had been erected. The bridge wasn't completed until after Brunel's death in 1859.

Jeremy Clarkson possibly did his best ever work on television when he climbed to the top of this exquisite structure to lobby viewers to support his case for Brunel being the greatest of great Britons. You voted Brunel number two after Winston Churchill.

Isambard bought some land near Torquay, where he aimed to retire with his family. But the stresses of his work overcame him. He had had a series of painful accidents over the years, as you might expect of someone who spent every day on building sites. And the trauma of the *Great Eastern* trials and tribulations severely debilitated him, as well as badly denting his finances. He died of a liver disease in 1859 and is buried at Kensal Green Cemetery.

What a legacy. Next time you take a train to or from Paddington, spare a few seconds to study the bronze of the genius viewing his terminus. I wonder what he would make of Heathrow and the M4.

That's enough Brunel. I've run out of steam.

28

Man-Made Motors

Before the First World War there were more than a hundred companies across Britain manufacturing motor vehicles.

It wasn't exactly a cottage industry. Rather it was generally a new line for established engineering firms: people who had been making horse-drawn vehicles, bicycles, motorbikes, railway components or factory engines. As soon as it became clear that the wealthy had a huge appetite for horseless carriages, many an entrepreneur turned their hand to it. After all, once you'd got your head around the basic principles of the internal combustion engine, it was merely a matter of designing and building a structure that seemed more appealing, reliable and efficient than the rest.

A hundred years on and there is virtually no home-grown car manufacture left in Britain. Yes, we service a handful of highly efficient plants for European or Japanese giants and we do operate Formula One design boutiques, but the regionally based, British-owned car production factory is a thing of the past – almost.

Every day of the week some lucky person climbs into the driver's seat of a brand new Morgan, starts it up and heads down a Worcestershire lane, thereby continuing a long and distinctive motoring tradition. Whoever has been able to invest the money and time in a new Morgan will have had the right to visit the factory at any time to watch the progress of their very own car. But this isn't an exclusive privilege for those who have paid their deposit. Anyone can have a look around this plant. It's open for unguided tours most mornings and afternoons. When I consider the hoops one has to clamber through to get near the factory floor at most premises, the Morgan Motor Company takes an almost perverse pleasure in being easy-going. unstructured and PR-free.

The prototype Morgan was a three-wheeler built for the 1910 motorcycle show at Olympia. It didn't attract much interest, as it was a single-seater. So H.F.S. Morgan reconfigured his proposition to provide a pair of seats, then he entered the vehicle in a string of rallies and races and built up a portfolio of successes. For example, at Brooklands in 1912 a Morgan was victorious in the Olympic one-hour cycle car race, breaking the world record by travelling 55 miles and 329 yards in precisely 60 minutes. What better incentive to acquire your own runabout for 85 guineas. The crossover to four wheels took place in the 1930s. The firm now points out that the 4/4 has been continuously produced for longer than any other car in the world.

To see one being assembled, just turn up at reception in Malvern, pay your £5 and you will be given a map of the site and a recommended route to follow. You can then wander through a series of old brick sheds where people are working individually at

their own pace and in their own way to put together one or another of the many variants and customised versions of a Morgan. It's refreshingly fundamental, and a telling contrast to brutally efficient production lines where whistling or smiling are perceived as acts of defiance to the management agenda.

The waiting list to purchase a Morgan is currently around five years. Time well spent, I'd say. And think of all those days when you can watch seasoned ash being carved into the essential framework for the body of your car.

If, like me, you have a strong nostalgic streak running through your veins, then the good news is there are plenty of places where you can indulge your need to drool over old motor cars. Many

The Morgan factory, in Worcester.

museums hold at least a few models from our motoring past, some just a single example. If you're in the West Midlands, don't miss the Kidderminster-manufactured 1921 three-wheeled Castle Three at Hartlebury Museum. If you're in Northern Ireland, nip into the Ulster Museum and track down the 1920s Chambers Open Tourer. The Chambers brothers were Belfast's only really successful car firm. They started in 1904 and built their own two-cylinder underflow engines with a chain drive to an epicyclical gearbox – which is perhaps why they went out of business in 1927.

There are lots of museums completely devoted to motor cars. How intriguing that we admire those crude, crazy, pioneering days of the freedom of the road, travelling to these temples in our contemporary vehicles on our contemporary roads – thereby furthering the devastating environmental impact that the internal combustion engine and its mass appeal have had on the world.

Nationally, summer sees lots of rallies for old cars and trucks. The Midlands seem particularly well served in this respect – probably because much of the manufacturing was based here and there is a legacy of appreciation of car production, plus an ability to fix bits that is no trouble at all to someone who might once have worked at Longbridge or Ryton. Coventry Transport Museum sits next to the bus station and is packed with examples of the magnificent range of motorised vehicles created in this city across a century. Many of the fundamental and iconic names of British manufacturing operated here – Alvis, Daimler, Jaguar, Hillman, Humber, Sunbeam, Standard and Triumph. For vans, buses and trucks, get up to Leyland in Lancashire and relish a day at the British Commercial Vehicle Museum. They even have a Popemobile and you can sit where the man himself once waved to the crowds.

For a reminder of a cute and curious world of personal motorised transport, beetle along to the British Bubblecar

Museum at Cranwell near Sleaford in Lincolnshire. Bubblecars are not covered motorbikes and they are not proper four-wheeled cars, they are tiny, tinny, toylike vehicles that make me think of aircraft cockpits on wheels – which is exactly how some of them developed from German aircraft factories such as Heinkel and Messerschmitt after the Second World War. British examples include the Bond – not the James, but the Laurie, of Lancashire, who produced microcars with a 650cc engine; and, of course, Del Boy's iconic Reliant Robin from *Only Fools and Horses*. (Personally I never really believed Del would ride round in one of these. He always seemed to me to be more of a knocked-off Cortina or

A carpenter working on the ash framework.

Capri man.) Jimmy Savile has lent his yellow BMW Isetta to the collection. It's customised and has a flashing yellow light on its roof. I'm told this model has two curious characteristics. First, it has a lever to move between three gears, first, second and top, and a separate lever to engage forward or reverse. So in theory you can get up to top gear in reverse. Secondly, it was quite easy for wags to sneak up on a stationary Isetta at traffic lights and just lift the rear drive-wheel off the ground. When the driver tried to pull away, he would put his foot down and the wheel and engine would roar, then the jokers dropped the chassis and the whirling wheel hit the road, spraying out burnt rubber until it got a grip on the surface and the little car screeched away.

There are seventy examples of minuscule machines with engines under 700cc at Cranwell. Perhaps they send a timely message to us now as we need to be thinking about more modest motoring in the future.

Another offshoot of military aircraft construction emerged in Bristol. The firm that had produced hundreds of vital Blenheims and Beaufighters for war service was suddenly at a loose end, so it set up a car division and within a year was offering its Type 400 Saloon to discerning customers. These beauties have never been cheap, boasting engineering and bodywork of a high order. They are still hand built near Filton, and their exclusiveness and obscurity seem only to add to their appeal.

In the garden with my sister, Anne.

Tony Dicken gave me a ride round the streets of Bristol in his restored 401 model dating from 1950. Tony was fortunate enough to find his machine derelict in an old garage and bought it for £1,500. He was also clever enough to be able to restore it, which took him nearly four years and gave him a magnificent end result worth £20,000.

Travelling in style in a Bristol 401.

29

Treasuring Trams

How is it that in the middle of the Peak District, right out in the country, we can take a ride on an Edwardian town tram any day of the week?

In the early years of the twentieth century every self-respecting city in Britain operated a tram system. This mechanised means of public transport was an import from America in Victorian times. Until their deployment we had been dependent on horse-drawn trams for mass transit in urban areas.

Trams utilised the railway principle of iron wheels turning efficiently when confined to metal tracks on a flat surface. The mechanised tram combined this with the exciting new power of electricity. Essentially a tram of this sort is a bogie system on rails with a big electric motor turning a pair of its wheels, on top of which is fixed a glorified wooden shed to accommodate passengers. The electricity is fed by an overhead wire.

The machines don't like corners and hills. They need long, flat, straight roads. This was ideal for the urban areas developing before the First World War. People could be moved between factory and home, city centre and suburb – without a trail of horse muck in the middle of the road.

Rather than having a huge turning circle at the end of each route, trams were designed to function in either direction. The driver's controls were sited at both ends of the vehicle, and many interiors had simple, flat wooden seats with backs that could be flipped to allow people always to face the direction of travel.

At their peak, in the 1920s, 14,000 trams were in service in Britain. But the advance of the internal combustion engine meant the tram routes began to lose out to buses, which could handle sharp corners and steep slopes, and didn't need cables strung through the air above them. And then, of course, along came private motoring. The tram's days were numbered.

When petrol seemed cheap, the tram lines were scrapped. Some of the passenger cabins were sold off as garden sheds and a few were saved for museums. Birmingham's Millennium Point has one of the city's old trams sitting adjacent to a steam locomotive, a Spitfire aircraft and the first Mini from Longbridge.

In 1948 Southampton joined the race to remove tram systems. A small group of tram enthusiasts watched the last machine with sadness. They couldn't bear to think of this curious two-storey, self-propelling carriage heading for the scrap heap, so they bought it – for £10. Now what?

They could find somewhere to display it, but they aspired to give the old girl more dignity. They wanted to provide her with some rails to call her own. Through the 1950s the Tramway Museum Society sought a location. and in 1959 heard about some old rails in a disused limestone quarry in Derbyshire. The

Crich quarry had been established by none other than the celebrated pioneer of British railway development, George 'Rocket' Stephenson, who had been commissioned to design and build the North Midland Railway to run from Derby to Leeds.

The route had required a tunnel through the Clay Cross hills. Halfway through the hillside the engineers encountered coal. Stephenson decided to use this to burn the local limestone for agricultural use and laid a track from the quarry works to Ambergate. It was this long corridor that proved the perfect place for the tram enthusiasts to deploy their preserved machines. They gathered track, cable and street furniture from all over the country, then erected the fabric of an urban street around their proud lines. They built replica buildings, not least the Derby Assembly Rooms, close to the track so visitors could get a sense of the typical circumstances in which the marvellous machines had functioned.

Which end's the front?

Glasgow Corporation tram number 22 had entered service in 1922 and ran until 1960, notching up about four million miles. She came to Crich in 1963, but – completely restored – made a brief return to the Scottish city in 1988 to transport the Royal Family around the Garden Festival. Chesterfield's number 7 tram entered service in 1904 and was retired in 1927, when the two decks were placed in a field next to each other to become a makeshift bungalow for an elderly lady. The museum recovered the wooden structure and restored it at a cost of £250,000. Now it's a proud member of the museum's fleet of sixty trams.

Yes, Blackpool still has its original trams, and half a dozen cities now operate an environmentally friendly contemporary fleet, but nowhere else in Britain can you travel back in time to the classic tram age. Go there and relish these fascinating icons of our transport history.

30

Road Rules

When Michael Palin makes a factual television programme, the chances are he flies to some foreign country, then takes a taxi to a railway station, where he will board an exotic express and spend the next week or so making observations about what he can see out the window.

Good luck to him. He does it immensely well.

Meanwhile on Planet Martin we are issued with a schedule that requires arrival at a valuation venue on a Sunday morning, an auction house on a Tuesday, Wednesday or Thursday, and some stately home, museum, collector's house or art studio somewhere within the United Kingdom on other days of the week.

The best logistical efforts are employed to minimise the inconvenience, cost and environmental impact of these journeys,

Paul Martin's Britain

The BBC provides me with chauffeur Graham so that I can undertake recording sessions close together. Health and safety rules mean they would have to factor in my motoring hours if I were to drive myself.

but the format of the show demands that I appear at these locations scattered across the map on time and in good form. Which is fine by me, because that's what I do and I take a pride in doing it.

Most of the time that I spend on the road, I'm in the back of a smart Mercedes, driven by Graham, who is contracted to move me around the country, cheerfully and intelligently. So I spend more time in Graham's company than many men do with their partners. Hence it's a good thing we get on very well.

Graham's professional interest lies in being a first-class driver, while my criterion is first-class presenting. Graham will sometimes make helpful suggestions about what I might say at a particular location. I welcome these observations, as the man has many years of television watching under his belt and so knows what makes for good viewing. I don't try to reciprocate, and never suggest he change gear or take a different route, which ensures harmony on the road.

If the radio is on it's generally tuned to Radio 2. Getting from the south-west to the north-east means hours in the company of Terry, Ken, Jeremy and Steve: amusing, informed, sparkling and spirit-lifting. Thank you, Radio 2.

Now Graham reckons he's a bit of an expert on pop music, and considerably more knowledgeable than me. I defer to his age. He's been around a good decade more than me so he's had time to hear more tunes. But I think my memory for and recognition of songs are superior. Every morning at 10.30, if it's a driving day, we can test our skills in Ken Bruce's Popmaster quiz questions. As Graham has his hands on the wheel, I do the totting up. Heading down the M6 one morning I had a call on my mobile phone from the *Flog It!* office. They wanted me to do a phone interview with a local radio station in an hour's time, talking about the show and flagging up the valuation day the next Sunday. I told the office to give the radio station my phone number.

BBC Radio Berkshire rang immediately. They were delighted I could do the chat, and were already announcing it to their listeners – Paul Martin would be on the show in an hour's time . . live. Then it dawned on me that this would clash with the quiz. Oh, conflict of interest, or what?

I pride myself on my professionalism, but my running feud with Graham over music memories was at a crucial point. I rang them back and told them I was in an area of very bad phone reception. We were passing through cuttings and tunnels, and I didn't want the signal to break up and spoil the interview. Their producer said I sounded fine. I abruptly switched the phone off, then rang back a minute later and asked her if she now appreciated the problem.

She said she understood, and so it was decided to move the interview on to a slot half an hour later, with a different radio presenter. Great – Graham and I could concentrate on our battle of the bands.

It was another close-fought contest as we headed along the motorway. Then Radio Berkshire rang again, and I said I was all set. I had a long on-air chat with the presenter. We talked about the show in general, my favourite types of antiques and what I knew about Berkshire. He then asked me where I was, and I told him we were heading south on the M6 in Staffordshire. He wasn't aware of any cuttings or tunnels along that stretch of motorway, he responded, and immediately my deceit was exposed. Oh dear.

I fudged my way out of this embarrassment implying we had only recently joined the motorway but I fear I was horribly unconvincing. I put down the phone feeling rather ashamed.

But it wasn't all bad. I had beaten Graham in the quiz by three points, which just goes to show that being older doesn't necessarily mean you hold more pop knowledge in your head.

31

In Fine Fettle

I love horses. I'm a huge fan of the beautiful animals that dignify the space they occupy and the way they move and look at you. It's extraordinary to think that a hundred years ago they were the primary means of transport power. Yes, horse power. Everyone with a business to run needed a horse to pull the cart or the plough, and rich folk had their carriages to be hauled. We were a rural economy, the greater part of the population tilling the soil. The move towards mechanisation and factory manufacture was gaining speed, but in 1907 more people were employed in agriculture than industry. Typical households in regional towns still relied on horse-drawn coal and milk carts until the 1950s.

Remember *Steptoe and Son*? Yes, the scrap-iron traders were a social anomaly in the 1960s, but only just. A decade earlier and

Mum giving me an early lesson.

their way of gathering unwanted metal would not have seemed out of place at all.

However, these days horses are a treat and a privilege and, thanks to my good fortune in becoming a five-days-a-week TV presenter, I've been able to buy a horse. He's called Jonny, a 4-year-old thoroughbred formerly known as Rebel Rouser in his racing days. Ever heard of him? No, of course not! He lost all his professional outings: 'poor chap, never really cottoned on to what it was all about.' That's where I come in – an unwanted 'gem for sale', at a fraction of his original value. Mind you, he came with a few issues and we found out the hard way: in mid-canter he would try his best to throw his rider off.

So off he went to Gary Witherford of Marlborough, a horse whisperer, a true master of natural horsemanship. If anyone could sort him out, then this was the bloke to do it. Watching Gary work with Jonny inside a huge galvanised ring was totally consuming: no tools or gimmicks, just a guy and a horse, a battle of egos and strength – another traditional skill and method that are sadly being overlooked and undervalued. And doing *Flog It!* has allowed me to explore the history and heritage of horses in a wide array of settings, from riding to carriage driving and ploughing fields, all while finding out more about my past heroes and more recent ones.

We were privileged to see a selection of exquisite paintings of George Stubbs at the Walker Gallery in Liverpool. He was a self-taught portrait painter from Liverpool who decided to get beneath the skin of his subjects. At the age of 21 he moved to York to study human anatomy at the County Hospital. A few years later he rented a farmhouse in Lincolnshire, where he could start dissecting horses. This led to his celebrated book, *The*

Anatomy of the Horse, and an immediate appreciation from the art and horse worlds that this man had a far better sense of the fine detail of the animal's structure than his predecessors. His career was now assured and he spent the rest of life completing commissions for wealthy and titled clients.

He wasn't totally hooked on horses, however, and sometimes headed off from his house in Marylebone to visit private zoos in order to tackle lions, tigers, giraffes, monkeys and rhinoceroses – in paint, that is.

Next let us trot elegantly over to the Red House Stables near Matlock, where I was given some memorable lessons in carriage driving from one of the country's leading experts, Caroline Dale-Leech, whose impeccable vehicles often feature in historical

In front of the old London to Edinburgh mail coach in Matlock, Derbyshire.

drama series on television. This means of transport may look great on screen, but it was arduous and uncomfortable, even assuming you didn't encounter a highwayman.

The master of capturing the lines and function of the horse in the first half of the twentieth century was Suffolk's Sir Alfred Munnings.

Alfred was the son of a miller from Mendham. He established a satisfactory reputation as a landscape painter, but he became fascinated by anatomy and meticulously studied the Stubbs stable of images. His wife, Violet McBride, was a committed rider and racehorse owner. She used her contacts to win her husband commissions, and Munnings was glad of the work. He laboured under a handicap, as you might say. He had lost the sight of one eye at the age of 20, hit in the face by a thorny branch while lifting his terrier over a stile. Munnings expert Ron Johns of Castle House near Colchester told me the disability did not affect Munnings's capacity to comprehend his subjects, but it did result in him often bringing too much pressure to bear on his paint-brush, as his lack of perspective meant he sometime failed to appreciate the distance of his hand from the canvas.

In 1944 Munnings became President of the Royal Academy, where he soon nailed his colours to the mast, and bluntly criticised modern art, not least the increasingly appreciated work of Picasso, which he described as shilly-shally painting. This position put him seriously out of fashion in the art world, and his elegant compositions were dismissed in some sniffy circles. But his ultimate significance in the history of horse painting is reflected in the fact that in recent years his canvases have changed hands for more than £4 million.

It's only a short ride from Castle House to Newmarket, and here we held a valuation day at the Tattersall sale rooms, and, of course, I had to pop into the National Horseracing Museum. The most compelling element of a marvellous exhibition is the tribute

Alfred J. Munnings,
*Study for the Yellow
Jockey*, oil on board.

to Victorian jockey Fred Archer, probably Britain's first sporting hero. By the time he was 29, in 1886, he had ridden in over 8,000 professional races, winning 2,748 of them, surely enough success to make him feel great?

Sadly, not all the time. He committed suicide that year with a handgun normally used for putting down injured animals. A combination of troubles sank his spirits. He had overstretched himself with a rather fancy house for his new wife, who lost their first child, then died herself during the birth of the second. At 5 feet 10 inches tall, Archer was not the normal diminutive build for a jockey, and struggled to keep his weight down to 8 stone 6 pounds. He took a special liquor to reduce his weight and it may be that an overdose of this caused him to jump off life's ride.

Riding stables, professional and amateur, are full of people with exceptional empathy for horses. The only other source of contemporary horse knowledge in the UK lies with the gypsy community. While all of them have moved on to motor vehicles, a few keep, appreciate and trade horses. I think I must have some gypsy in my blood to sustain my line of work – nomadically criss-crossing the country. Whenever I get the chance, I'll always talk to gypsies about their horses. It's a great ice-breaker with a group of people who so frequently feel marginalised. I've enjoyed visits to gypsy sites and seen wonderful examples of carefully restored old caravans and met the horses that proudly pull them down quiet country lanes. Great examples of fine wooden caravans can be seen at the Worcestershire County Museum and at the Gordon Boswell Romany Museum in Lincolnshire.

I was given a guided tour of Gordon Boswell's wonderful collection of Romany artefacts. Gordon was born in a tent and remembers well his family travelling in their wooden caravan along country lanes. They would do four hours in the morning, rest the horse for four hours, then do another three or four hours. That would typically take them 25 miles. High up on the caravan they could see across fields and spot business opportunities, like scrap metal. They built and decorated the caravans them-selves, and put carpet on the interior of the roof for insulation, running a wood stove inside for night-time heat. They lived off things that others threw away. Are you thinking what I'm thinking? This was sustainable living before Friends of the Earth ever existed. Gordon's mum did fortune telling, many a Romany having this gift. His dad built a caravan at the age of 70, and this is the cornerstone of the collection that Gordon pulled together.

We harnessed up Billy the horse and I enjoyed a romantic, magical ride on a beautiful wagon, drawn by a beautiful horse along a beautiful country lane.

Once a jockey has stopped riding winners at the major race tracks, what does he do next? Become a trainer or stable manager?

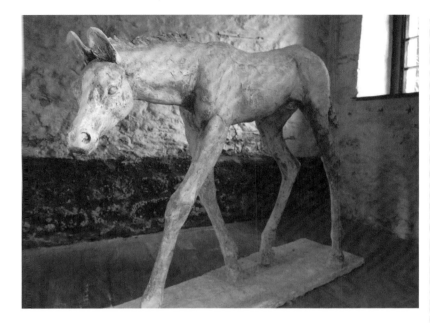

A full-size plaster model of a foal by Phil Blacker, from which he created a bronze casting. I fell in love with this in his studio, and just had to own it.

Or get out of the field altogether. Footballers who fail to make a fortune from Premiership exposure can take up sports coaching or run a shop. What about a jockey? Well, there's only room for a couple of television commentators on the topic, and I see no change in those roles for the foreseeable future. After winning the Derby once and the Cheltenham Gold Cup three times, jockey Phil Blacker made a big, distinctive and highly successful leap from the saddle.

He now sculpts horses.

Being married to an art teacher was a key factor in this. Phil had a sophisticated appreciation of the representation of these wonderful animals in two dimensions. Could he capture the lines and character of an individual horse in lifelike proportions? He set out to try and, after many months of trial and error with clay, started to develop the skills that allowed him to shape the material into a form that reflected for him and others the precise contours of these handsome creatures. Now Phil and his skills are in great demand. Many racecourses are graced by one of his big bronze pieces: Aintree sports Phil's *Red Rum*, Epsom and Kempton Park proudly display a Blacker animal, and I know he is currently working on a life-size *Best Mate* to grace another racecourse..

He begins by erecting and welding a steel superstructure and moulds clay on to this. When the shape of the animal is complete, a plaster of Paris mould is made and then a bronze cast can be formed using the lost wax method.

Phil has a list of orders for private commissions, which don't come cheap. If you have a horse that you would like to see immortalized in bronze, Phil can satisfy your requirements for around £125,000, some of which is spent on the one and a half tons of clay necessary.

On the outskirts of Windsor I visited the Royal Berkshire Polo Club and was rather taken with what I discovered there. Riding a horse is a skill in itself. Combining this with accurately hitting a small hard ball with a long thin mallet seems impossibly problematic, but hundreds of people tackle the task and some are highly successful. The Royal Family bring glamour and status to the sport, and people with time and money endeavour to flourish in the activity.

I took some lessons – indoors. How can this be, you ask. Well, imagine a room with a wooden horse in the middle of it. Then instead of the floor spreading out flat and evenly to the bottom of the walls, think of a floor that slopes upwards as it moves away from the horse. So the horse is in effect sitting in a shallow, straight-sided pit. Now you've got the essential configuration for an indoor polo training facility. You get on your horse (galloping effect optional), take hold of your mallet, and hit the small ball on the floor. Wherever and however you strike it, it will roll back towards the horse within seconds, and so you swing at it again – simple as that.

Charlotte and Jonny.

If you do this for about a month, you might be sufficiently proficient to emerge from the dark, go out on to a polo field and not look a complete prat. Who said 'That's impossible'?

A big thank you to proprietors Mark and Sam for a very special day out that I will never forget.

32

Bonkers

ou've heard me use this term. I was describing a collector. It sounds condemnatory, dismissive, rude. But admiration is implied as well.

Naturally, at some time or other during the process of putting together their extraordinary collection, someone – friend, neighbour, work colleague, as well as family members – will have called them bonkers. But they have persevered and organised and contextualised, and become an expert in their field, someone who is sought after and highly regarded for their exceptional knowledge and remarkable specialist mini-museum.

The fact is that many have been the subject of a five-minute film on BBC2 along with some of Britain's foremost examples of social and industrial heritage. So let's respect them and treasure them. The crazy, committed, single-minded collectors.

What are the criteria for becoming a bonkers collector? You must have an obsession, time and money. But there's more to it than that. Collecting stamps, coins, railway locomotive numbers, cigarette cards, beer-mats, pens or postcards requires the above characteristics, but essentially such collectables fail to pass the bonkers bar because they are just too ordinary.

Cigarette cards, for example, were designed for collecting. You opened your packet of Gallaher's cigarettes to find, alongside the fags, a small card with a colour picture of a layout of dominos on one side and text on the other, which was headed 'Tricks and Puzzles Series No. 51, Removing the Domino'. There follow instructions on how to perform the trick and thus amaze and delight your friends. The card is one of 100 in the set. What an incentive to buy many more packets of cigarettes in order to acquire the whole collection. Statisticians will understand that purchasing 1,000 packets still does not guarantee completing the set, but if you invested in 100 then you could swap cards until you had every number and thus every puzzle in the series.

So cigarette cards were designed for – well, not collecting, but to get you to smoke more of a particular brand. And we can lump the stamps and coins and so on in the same common or garden collecting territory.

The bonkers collectors have gone for something gob-smacking. A subject that is bizarre, ridiculous, problematic. Something immensely obscure or horribly open-ended.

Let's start with the latter. At an auction in north Wales I met a man bidding for an old cast-iron mangle. What would he want with this, I wondered? To add to his collection. He already had a dozen, but this was a different model from any of the rest. Mangles were merely a tiny part of Pat's vast, eclectic collection of household objects of the twentieth century. In a pub quiz in 1974 he had won a tea mug with a panel advertising Rich Tea biscuits on the side. This inspired him to start collecting more examples of tea mugs. Now he has 1,400. From there he decided to branch out – in more or less every direction. Now he has 3,000 square metres of space devoted to, well, stuff. Bus stops, mechanical fly sprays, hand-pumped vacuum cleaners, gas masks, hair dryers, shoe cleaning kits. Get the picture?

He is not alone. At Hermitage Hall near Downham Market, south of King's Lynn, Eric has had the space, money and passion to collect an enormous range of artefacts of the twentieth century, big and small. In his transport department he has some carts, some carriages, some cars and a Concorde engine. He pointed out to me that one should collect wisely to capture the past, and pursue only those things for which one has a passion and an enthusiasm. He's particularly proud of his original letters of Admiral Lord Nelson, who came from this area. Not all the letters reveal the same handwriting. Eric explained that the early ones were penned with the great sailor's right hand; when he lost his arm, he learned to write with his left hand.

Eric's favourite item is a pair of old cinema seats. On his honeymoon at Lynmouth he took his wife to see *Wuthering Heights*. When that cinema was being demolished, Eric bought the two front circle seats and gave them to his wife as a fiftieth wedding anniversary present.

OK, the above are generalists. Now let's meet a cross-section of specialists.

Many households have hung on to their record collection. Some people have hung on to music-making machinery. In Bradford, Phil and Pam have an enormous collection of free reed harmoniums (or should that be harmonia?). Great big boxes that reproduce music by triggering tuned blowers from the patterns on a paper roll, driven by hand, foot, clockwork or electricity.

In Chichester an old Methodist church is stuffed full of mechanical musical instruments of all sorts. Record players through the ages, tunes typically triggered by a scatter of teeth emerging from a metal disc.

There are dozens of places around the country that people can visit and hear music being made or reproduced by all sorts of means. However, for crazy commitment, I defy you to top Frank James, who has filled his Herefordshire farmhouse living room with two particular makes of gramophone dating from the 1920s, complete with their giant papier-mâché horns, which were apparently unrivalled for sound reproduction qualities. The EMG and Expert horns are nearly 2 metres long and, at their mouths, a metre in diameter. Frankly, it's not easy to move around the room without bumping into one, and when it comes to dusting – don't ask. Let's just say that Mrs James is one of the most tolerant women a man could hope to meet.

Who does the ironing in your household? Our contemporary electric-powered steam irons are so sophisticated that they almost do the ironing themselves (an automatic iron – wouldn't that be a popular invention?). At the start of the twentieth century, gas-powered irons were the latest domestic convenience. You lit the gas in a little burner behind the heavy flatplate, which was con-

His Master's Voice.

nected to the mains gas supply by a big rubber tube. Might seem madness now, but it was state-of-the-art technology at the time. Ken Faulkner gets a place in my bonkers album by having collected 650 different models of gas irons dating between 1890 and 1920. I'm sure he doesn't dare ask Mrs Faulkner to do his shirts.

Collecting cars is a very popular specialism. On a manageable, non-bonkers level, let's face it, many men are boys who haven't really grown up and who cannot bear to part with their Dinky or Corgi toys. We see many a collection appear on *Flog It!* valuation days. But for people with more space and more money there are bigger prospects.

Many of you will never have heard of the Humber. This was a luxury motor car produced in Coventry between 1932 and 1976. Alan Marshall loved them and started to collect them. He's got forty-seven, including the one that Edward VIII (the 325-day king) used for taking Mrs Simpson on surreptitious dates before they admitted to their affair in 1936. Bet the chauffeur could have told some tales. But he didn't.

If you've haven't got the appetite, or the room for that matter, for dozens of cars, what about two-wheelers? Nigel Cox's Lambretta Museum in Weston-super-Mare holds every model the firm made from 1947 until 1970. That's sixty-five old motor scooters. Many were rescued from scrap, and, restored, they are worth thousands of pounds.

Militaria is a highly specialised subject for collecting, with some big fans and a few possibly unhinged enthusiasts. One man who convinced me he wasn't off his rocker was Richard Ashley. In 1918 at the age of 5 he received from the War Office a cardboard box full of his uncle's possessions. His uncle had been an officer in the First World War, and so Richard inherited his uniform, bayonet and other field equipment. This stimulated him to start collecting the artefacts of face-to-face warfare, which make for a gruesome and sobering sight – and a reminder, as Richard pointed out, of the horrors of war, and why it should be avoided at all costs. Richard has examples of German barbed wire, and of a British device designed to fit on a rifle and fire a bullet through the wire in order to break it. Just think, this was considered a brilliant invention less than a hundred years ago.

I've recalled a few of the people who can't bear to part with anything from their homes. Inevitably they've usually got half a dozen phones on their shelves, reflecting the evolving technology of person-to-person telecommunication.

In Brighton I called up Shane, who has collected phones and only phones. And phones being phones, he's naturally connected some of them up so he can ring himself on a different instrument and talk to himself down the line. He's even got an exchange machine and one of those old phone box coin containers with the A and B buttons for putting your four pennies in to allow you to make a call, then, once you'd got through to the other party, committing them to the cash tray below.

Then there is Dennis White's beautiful bonkers collection of oil lamps. Ramsbury is a sweet little village in Wiltshire, and Dennis is a charming local man, whose parents ran one of the general stores that used to service the high street. He remembers as a child being employed to help at the counter and take deliveries to people's homes on the shop's dedicated bicycle. Dennis witnessed the arrival of piped gas, then electricity, to Ramsbury. Suddenly there was light on demand. Previously everyone had depended on individual oil lamps, containers of paraffin feeding fuel to a wick inside a glass chimney. The oil lamp was lit at night and provided modest illumination for those in its vicinity.

As gas and electricity caught on, Dennis remembers seeing oil lamps being thrown out with the rubbish: they no longer had a purpose. He thought it was a shame to see them scrapped and so started to gather them up. When his parents' shop eventually closed down, Dennis was at a loose end. What should he do with himself? He decided to make good all the old lamps he had collected. He would clean them up, find new pieces for broken parts and present them in the best possible light.

He turned the family grocery shop into a home for his collection, and gradually became one of the country's leading specialists in the field. Now Inglenook Antiques attracts enthusiasts from all over Britain who want to buy or sell an oil lamp. Dennis was doubtless branded bonkers by someone in Ramsbury long ago, but now he has created a celebrated centre of excellence and a tourist attraction for his village.

Imagine you bought an old house in Shropshire, and started to dig over the garden and discovered fragments of clay pipes in the soil. What would you do? Why, keep on digging, of course.

This is what Rex Key did and, in the process, steadily uncovered not just dozens of bits of clay pipe but hundreds, then thousands, and then tens of thousands. This was because – as he eventually learnt – his garden lay right on top of what had been the discard site for a Victorian clay-pipe factory.

Anyone from Shropshire will realise that the house must have been in the village of Broseley near Ironbridge on the River Severn, because this was a huge centre of clay-pipe making in the nineteenth century.

Now another man might have considered the fragments of pipe in the garden a considerable nuisance and a potential limitation to horticultural prospects. But Rex was delighted with his finds, and judiciously cleaned and sorted every piece that emerged from the soil. The rich underground seam of pipe pieces stimulated Rex to learn more about the history and processes of pipe making in the area. There were three major manufacturers, the primary producers being R. Smitheman and Co. of King Street. Piece-workers, mostly female, would turn out at least 600 pipes a day.

The luxury pipe, affectionately known as the churchwarden's pipe.

Paul Martin's Britain

Almost the whole population smoked in Victorian times and cigarettes had yet to be popularised. Short clay pipes would be stuffed with strands of tobacco leaf and puffed on at every opportunity. The well-to-do enjoyed a pipe with a longer stem, to stop the smoke and nicotine getting in their eyes and up their noses. The longest stems were 22 inches (that's more than half a metre). These were the churchwarden pipes, so called because only the idle church officials had the time to smoke them.

As well as conferring status, the longer-stemmed pipe had a further advantage – it allowed your hands to be free. Yes, a short pipe had to be held, and cupped. You might hold it briefly in your teeth, but the fragile finish would probably result in you accidentally biting through the stem and so losing the bowl and your precious tobacco. If you could run to a long stem, then you could rest the bowl on a table, leaving your hands free to write a letter or play a game of cards, or whatever the gentleman smoker might wish to do to occupy himself beyond and around the fug he was creating in front of his face.

Rex has taken his enthusiasm for this activity to the maximum. He helped establish a pipe museum in Broseley, and here, as well as being able to examine every conceivable variety of clay pipe, you can have a go at making one. Wouldn't that be a good thing to do for a *Flog It!* Insert: Paul has a go at pipe making.

Yes, I was given instruction in the art from Rex. You roll out a pancake of clay, then form it into a tube around a thick wire. Carefully draw the wire out of the tube and it becomes hollow. Now you've got your stem, which, with a bit of slip (wet clay), can be joined to the bowl. Not easy, but achievable. And so I put one together in front of the camera.

And Rex very kindly said he would bake the pipe and send it to me. Which he did – in time for our valuation day at Shrewsbury's Old Music Hall. It turned up by special delivery. Carefully nestled in bubble wrap inside an old shoe box, there was the churchwarden's pipe I had rolled, and which Rex had fired.

To test a pipe for smokability, one option is to stick some tobacco in the bowl, light it and suck hard on the cancer-inducing smoke. No, not a good idea. The other technique is to squirt some washing-up liquid into the bowl and then blow down the stem. If the airway is sound, bubbles should emerge from the bowl. Great fun.

I unwrapped the pipe and laid it carefully on the chair next to me at the valuation day. I was checking my script when one of the *Flog It!*

Another pipe break, this time in the Broseley workshop.

researchers, Nick Denning, came over for a very important meeting. It was to ask me what I would like for lunch. Nick moved on, continuing with this vital task across the whole crew, and I returned to my pipe – now in pieces on the chair. Nick had sat on it.

We had to roll stickytape around the segments of stem, before pouring washing-up liquid into the bowl. All credit to the stickytape makers – bubbles emerged from the bowl on cue.

I've got a rack of clay pipes in my bathroom now, not for smoking, just for decoration. Try it – it has a nice, manly look. You can get a complete churchwarden's pipe at auction for around £100. One tip: don't ever leave it on a chair when someone's lurking around with a lunch menu.

And here our enlightening tour of bonkerism comes to a happy end.

33

Sunset Skills

I respect man's capacity to find ingenious new ways to tackle traditional tasks, and I'm not a Luddite who resists progress and rejects technical advance, but it's always a pleasure to encounter craftsmen and women who have learned the classical means of manufacturing something and continue to pursue those ways, whatever pressures the marketplace puts on the economics of their endeavours.

Among my visits to workshops where traditional techniques are honourably applied, I have particularly heart-warming memories of a visit to Sheffield.

Question: why would Elvis Presley want a penknife? No, I can't think of a reason either. He wasn't a Boy Scout type who might wish to do a bit of whittling by a bonfire. To the best of my

knowledge he didn't go trout fishing and so need a means of cutting line or bait. And from what I know of his lifestyle, the chances are he would have teams of people to sharpen his pencils in the event that he ever had a pencil that required sharpening. Yet I can say with confidence that the King of Rock and Roll had a penknife. Because I know the man who made it.

Stan Shaw is a master cutler and one of the last remaining independent knife-makers in Britain. As you might expect, he's based in Sheffield, which, of course was the world's number one centre of knife-making until late in the twentieth century. Why would someone want one of Stan's knives as opposed to any other? Because they are entirely hand made, individual works of art and craft, precisely constructed, great to look at, lovely to hold and exceptionally effective. Mr Presley would not settle for less.

Stan got into knife making in 1940. Some of Sheffield's manufacturing was being retooled to deal with munitions production, but there were still around 8,000 people employed in the cutlery trade. Factories full of dedicated craftsmen produced the steel that became blades used for every type of knife from butter to butchery. At 14 Stan had just left school, and so he walked up to the front door of a big cutlery factory and asked if he could please make knives. They welcomed him in and he became an apprentice, spending the next six years acquiring an understanding of every aspect of the work. In parallel with the mass-produced output, there was always an appetite for one-offs, which the factory business didn't want to undertake. Instead the firms would rent small amounts of workshop space to cutlers – typically a yard of bench – which would allow them, in their own time, to proceed with individual orders.

Stan served many years in major factories, sharpening his skills, dare I say. In the 1970s the British cutlery industry started to be hit by cheap foreign imports, so Stan began to concentrate on his personal work, and to specialise in pocket knives and penknives.

Opposite: Master cutler Stan Shaw at the workbench.

Paul Martin's Britain

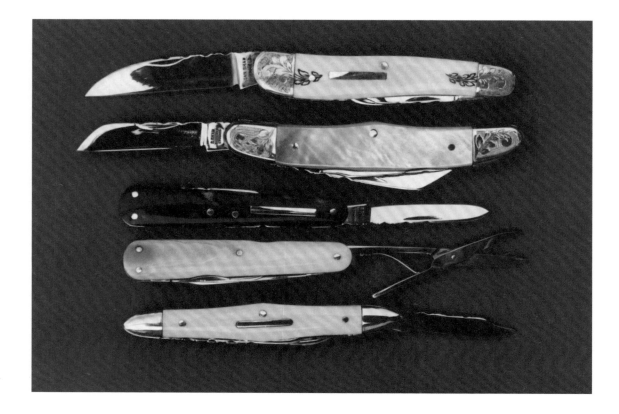

A selection of the knives
that Stan Shaw has
produced over the years.

A penknife traditionally had just one blade; its job was singular – to trim the quill of an ink pen, which would slowly blunt as a gentleman or his clerk wrote letters or notes. The pocket knife has a pair of blades – one a short pen-trimming blade, the other longer, for general purposes. There was some British production of multi-tooled devices, but the Swiss stitched up this segment of the market with their complicated contraptions combining everything from corkscrews to tweezers in a weighty instrument.

This left Stan and some fellow entrepreneurs to concentrate on the classic: the pocket knife, hand-tooled with a range of appropriate natural finishes – horn, bone, leather, hoof, mother-of-pearl. Even the springs for each blade are made individually. Stan is now in his seventies and is the only remaining master

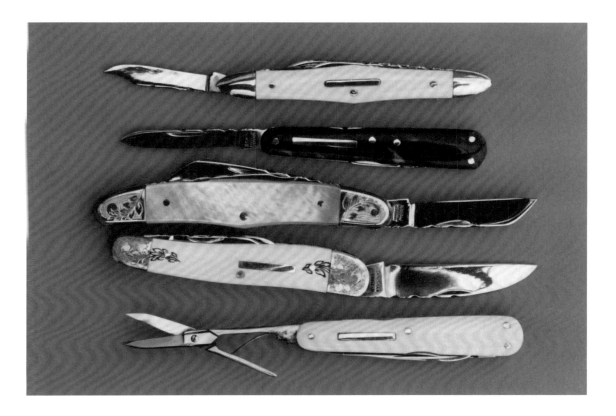

cutler plying this trade. He occupies a wonderful old workshop that could be a museum piece in its own right.

He has no assistant, or, more critically, apprentice. And so when he retires these marvellous skills will no longer be available. The irony is it's not a dying business. Stan has orders that will keep him busy for the next four years.

It takes him a couple of months to produce his special knives. Some of them cost more than a £1,000. He does no advertising. He's reluctant even to post finished products to customers. He prefers people to call in, and take their knife away in person. Hence the appeal for people who want something exclusive.

Sheffield has always been a popular venue for pop bands. Rock musicians have an appetite for the curious, rare and special. By word of mouth, groups heard of Stan's special knives. Suddenly Swiss Army combos seemed run of the mill. The boys in the bands wanted a Stan Shaw special – and so they kept him busy. And one of his finest knives was bought as a gift for Elvis. It was taken to Gracelands by a guitarist who regularly worked with the blue-suede-shoed one. And the feedback for Stan was that 'The Pelvis' treasured his present from Sheffield.

When did man first learn to sail? Egyptian illustrations show sailing boats on the Nile, so we know we were at it 4,000 years ago, but I'm sure the principle of holding a piece of cloth to capture the wind and so drive a vessel along had been discovered thousands of years before then.

Now we have fibreglass craft with carbon fibre masts and Kevlar sails. But the principles of sailing still stand. Fix a mast into your boat, attach a sheet of material to it, then manipulate the loose end to harness the wind and manoeuvre yourself across the water.

Contemporary sail making is a factory activity, but I was delighted on my visit to Mersea Island to moor up next to a traditional sail-maker, John Benz. He's been at it for fifty years. He was trained to handle canvas and hemp rope to produce all the necessary sails for fishing smacks plying the Thames estuary. Now most of those boats have gone (though he has inherited one himself) and very few sailors require the old-fashioned materials. John and his colleagues can knock up a new synthetic sail in about four hours, whereas hand sewing thick, heavy hemp and canvas takes four days. John's traditional skills are in danger of disappearing. He points out he cannot afford to employ an apprentice to acquire this craft when it's only once or twice a year that there is a demand for such exclusive abilities. I watched John create the cord grommets and then hammer home the metal eyelet on to a jib sail that was to become a replacement aboard a weather-damaged wooden-hulled schooner. Who's going to be able to do this sort of thing once John and his team are gone?

I would have loved to go out to sea on the boat, but that's something that the *Flog It!* Insert schedule seldom allows. When you have more stuff to shoot in the afternoon, the last thing you want is the crew and presenter stuck out at sea waiting for the wind to change.

On the edge of the Savernake Forest Bill Cook earns a good living carving wood. This is because he applies his art and eye in a very specialised field – replacing damaged or missing elements of antique furniture.

If worm or clumsiness has destroyed the leg of a chair, for example, Bill will examine what's left and then set forth to produce what is missing. I watched with awe when he tackled an intricately carved clawed foot. This chair had completely lost the bottom half of its walnut cabriole right leg; the left leg, however, was sound. Bill dug out a chunk of walnut of the same period as the chair itself – the early eighteenth century – and perfectly glued this lump on to the upper part of the broken leg. He then commenced carving the walnut so that it slowly started to become a match for the left leg. This took him the best part of a day. His tools are razor-sharp and he works with care and confidence. He explained that he needs to have a feel for the eye of the original carver in order to replicate that carver's hand. He has to see the curve, to see the hand. The most critical point is when attempting to blend the new piece of wood invisibly into the original section. Here he deploys a sharp cabinet scrape (a thin piece of steel with a sharp edge) and draws it carefully over the joint line of the leg exactly as the original craftsman would have done two hundred years ago.

Bill had an eight-year apprenticeship, but considers he never stops learning. Thankfully his sons are working in the business and acquiring Bill's expertise. He truly is an artist and a master craftsman. Let's hope the sun will never set on such skills.

34

What Would You Do, Paul?

Every time I go into a supermarket someone will tell me how much they like *Flog It!*, someone will want my autograph (twice on the side of a breakfast cereal packet!) and someone will want me to tell them what will make a profit in the world of collectables.

The first two encounters are a pleasure, but the third one is a problem. The answer is that I don't know.

No one knew that Troika and Clarice Cliff would grow and grow in appeal, and that meanwhile brown furniture would take a dreadful dive. If I had been smart and market-oriented and able to see into the future, I would have sold all my antique furniture and instead filled a shed full of Troika. If maximising my wealth was my single aim, that is. Fact is, I love my brown furniture, and if it

Signing an autograph for Gran.

has dropped in commercial value, then the good thing for me is I can buy more of it, and every piece is a joy to look at and a privilege to own.

Good furniture has a symmetry and exquisite scale. It's like an architectural achievement in wood. Classic cabinet-makers apply 50 per cent art and 50 per cent geometry to their task, and the subsequent owners of the chair or table or cabinet have the pleasure of that craft in their eye for all time.

When I ran my shop, I took great joy in perfecting my weekly display. I would buy during the early part of the week and spend Thursday night or Friday morning preparing my new pieces for the weekend. A good tip is to visit antiques shops on a Friday when the new pieces have arrived. That way you'll see them first. However, if you try to horsetrade, the dealer may hold back because he or she can anticipate more customers turning up in the next twenty-four hours.

I was always happy to achieve a sale – not simply to get some more cash in my hand, but for the pleasure I provided to that customer. The Buddhists believe that by giving something away you get something back. Well, I didn't give things away in my shop (though it sometimes felt like that), but I was certainly getting more than cash in return. And any decent antiques dealer puts store by such experiences.

Now in my home I treasure a portfolio of historical objects about which I have learnt what I can. It's such a privilege to look at and touch these possessions, and to be aware of their place in our rich social history. The sensation can make my tummy flutter.

Oh, all right, I'm avoiding a satisfactory answer to the original question. With the proviso that this was never going to be a book of tips, here are a few I can offer you.

Buy what you like, and go for quality. Look for the maker's name and marks, and avoid damage. Spend as much as you can afford. Yes, fashions change, but the best examples won't fall as far or as fast.

Don't buy something that's restored and don't unnecessarily clean antiques.

Original oil paintings are good, if they are signed and dated, and there is no evidence of tampering with the frame. Subject-wise, pretty girls command the highest prices.

Avoid silver and gold – they are troublesome and attract bad company. It's

Not a patch on SpongeBob!

easy to be fooled, and it's easy to lose precious metal. I'm told Victorian and Edwardian diamonds can be bought very cheaply and can be recut and remounted into a modern piece of jewellery, but this is highly specialised. You really need to know what you're doing.

As with every field, read and learn. Ask experts, watch television shows, surf the Internet and add to your knowledge.

Despite the inexplicable decline in value of early eighteenth-century oak and mahogany furniture, I would personally recommend trying to find a single Chippendale chair.

Buy it, look at it, sit on it and treasure it. And never think of flogging it. Let it make you very happy by its presence in your life.

35

Being James May

I have fond memories of my visit to York, when we held a
valuation day at the racecourse, and I had an opportunity to
look round the magnificent Minster. This is a beautiful
building in a beautiful city. I found the interior inspiring and
uplifting. As I gazed at aspects of the chancel I felt I was looking
up into the heavens. The stained-glass windows confirmed for me
that God is Light.

Sunday morning was a chance not to attend a Minster service,
but instead make the short journey from my excellent hotel near
the racecourse to the valuation. As I emerged from the foyer I
witnessed a cheerful gentleman handing a fifty-pound note to the
doorman. I commented light-heartedly that people tip generously
around here. The doorman explained that he had just cleaned the

Paul Martin's Britain

Filming at Pinewood
studios on Stanley Long's
project, *The History of
Pinewood.*

gentleman's car windscreen. Windscreen? I would want several complete car valets for that sort of money. The gentleman now turned to me and said: 'I love your programme. Always watch it.' I thanked him and took a step towards my car, which Graham had brought to the front of the building. But my fan took me by the arm and said: 'Come and have a look at my car.'

He was parked close to the lobby entrance. And now I could see why he was prepared to invest £50 in a screen clean. It was a brand new Bentley Continental GT, about £135,000 worth of motor vehicle, in a slate grey, the first model made for the UK market.

Stanley telling me how to deliver my lines. Double Oscar winner Jack Cardiff OBE, Director of Photography, still working in his nineties, looks on from his chair.

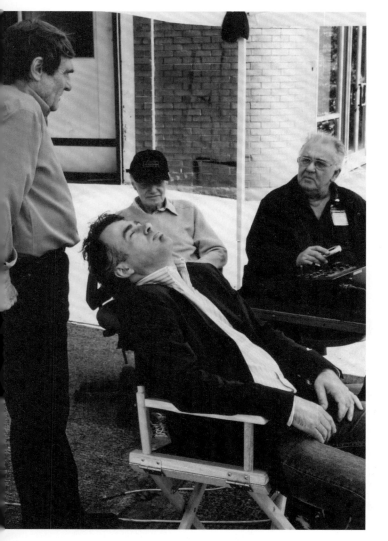

It's been a hard day.

'What do you think of it?' the chap asked.

Well, what do you say? 'Wonderful,' I replied.

'Would you like to feature it on the programme?'

'We certainly haven't had anything like this on the show,' I observed.

'No, you haven't,' he replied, obviously familiar with most episodes. 'This is the first model made available to the market.'

'We had a three-wheeled bubble car in Peterborough.'

He looked at me quizzically. He must have missed this one.

'And there was the Morris Minor Traveller in Suffolk.'

Again he seemed surprised.

'And, of course, the *Bristol* in Bristol.'

'Oh, yes.'

I felt he hadn't seen this Insert film either, but was trying to be knowing and friendly.

'Take a spin in it,' he suggested.

I had Graham standing by to drive me to the valuation, where there were probably 500 people waiting to see me, plus an anxious director keen to do some opening links outside the building before allowing the queue to move inside.

It was tempting to stay a little longer here and be driven round the block in this extremely up-market motor.

And now the fellow handed me the keys.

Oh, my goodness, he was going to let me drive his luxury machine. Was this wise? Surely not. Still, if he could afford a car like this, I'm sure he could maintain a first-class car insurance policy, and not worry too much about losing his no-claims bonus.

Should I delay my arrival at the valuation to spend five minutes behind the wheel of this glorious limo?

I then thought I could drive it to the valuation and bemuse the crew, who would think I had perhaps just bought the Bentley out of what they imagine to be my inflated fees.

That would be a great wind-up.

I put my hand out to take the keys from the chap as he said: 'Always think you do a much better job than that Clarkson fellow.'

So, he wasn't a *Flog It!* fan. He was a *Top Gear* addict, and I assume must have taken me for James May. Similar long hair, though his is a lot messier than mine, I like to think. And James is about six inches taller than me. As I took the keys, I caught Graham's eyes. He was shaking he head and mouthing: 'No, not a good idea.' For a split second I thought this was a really good idea. I could take this for a spin, and if I did have a prang I could hand back the keys saying, 'Send the bill to *Top Gear!*' Well I liked the idea of being James May.

Back at the hotel that evening I discovered that the man was the film director Stanley Long, who had made a number of British features in the 1970s. Later he found out who I was and, feeling guilty, wanted to apologise. So he contacted my agent to get my phone number and two or three weeks later he rang me. It turned out he was a great *Flog It!* fan and also a fan of my presenting. He explained he was a retired film director who was using all his contacts to make a film about the history of Pinewood Studios, where he had been based, and he wanted me to present it. So I ended up working for him and becoming a good friend.

36

The Beat Lives On

'Congratulations!' sang a good-looking, stylish young man to me and my mum and dad. 'Congratulations!' repeated the teen heart-throb, causing a crowd of pretty girls to swoon. 'Congratulations!' came once again the refrain from the mouth of Britain's competitor in the Eurovision Song Contest.

And 'Congratulations!' was the reply, because Cliff Richard won the event with this number – which I, my mum and my dad, along with fourteen million other Brits, and a considerable proportion of the population of Europe, heard that Saturday night in 1968.

'You could be another Cliff Richard,' remarked my mum, bless her, always seeing me as having showbiz potential. I didn't point out that I couldn't sing, but no matter. On that evening Cliff

Paul Martin's Britain

Opposite: Cliff, Paul and Stanley Long, who has been John Mills's neighbour for twenty years.

became a reference point for my childish ambitions and aspirations. Years later, when I was a teenager, some of my enduring heroes in the world of rock music were the super-group Yes, led by keyboard player Rick Wakeman. That band ticked all the boxes for me when I reached my teens. I loved the album covers, admired the art and bowed in deference to everything associated with Rick Wakeman and Co. Oh, yes, and he could sing.

Twenty-five years later a funny thing happened. Out of the blue I was invited to unveil a blue plaque for English Heritage identifying the house in which the late Sir John Mills had lived in Denham. The unveiling would take place at the house at eleven o'clock one Sunday morning in Denham village. And guess what? I would not have to undertake the task alone. Doubtless to give the occasion a greater sense of, well, occasion, they were going to bring along a proper celebrity. Who would this be, I wondered.

I was told to be at the house at 10.30 a.m. to have a little practice before the photographers arrived. I'd mugged up on Sir John Mills, his illustrious career and filmography, and realised the value of a rehearsal in case my speech overlapped with that of the other celebrant. I decided to concentrate on Sir John's place in film history and his contribution to British culture, with perhaps a few words about the delights of Denham. One of the delights of Denham is that it does not bend over backwards to accommodate the motorcar. Car-parking is distinctly limited and the pavements are not structured to deal with hordes of strangers. The only time there is a crowd in Denham is when the Sunday morning church service comes to an end, and, of course, this was the very moment when we were due to declare Sir John's plaque well and truly unveiled.

But with whom would I be sharing the task?

I drove past the house, where I could see an anxious woman pacing around below a curious temporary external curtain above the door. I parked as close as I could – probably half a mile away –

and hurried back towards the organiser. Thankfully she recognised me. I mumbled something about the parking. 'Mercifully Cliff's being chauffeur-driven,' she explained.

'Cliff,' I thought. I wondered . . . and the next moment a big car pulled up and out hopped a good-looking, stylish man – the same one who had won the Eurovision Song Contest thirty years earlier.

We were introduced and the English Heritage hostess gave us a quick explanation of the procedure. It would be a shared task. Who would speak first? Cliff, of course. I couldn't wait to tell my mum: at long last I was another Cliff Richard.

I racked my brains to recall whether John Mills might have had an undocumented cameo part in *Summer Holiday*. Seemed unlikely. Meanwhile the others decided I should go first. So I wasn't really another Cliff. I was in fact Cliff's warm-up act. OK, Mum, I came close.

Anyway, by now a crowd was gathering, and lots of photographers were setting up in the road itself to get shots of Cliff adjacent to the plaque. The church service had ended and so Denham's pinched streets and footpaths were now utterly overwhelmed. Half the people were showbiz enthusiasts – here to see and celebrate Sir John, Cliff, the British film industry and maybe even little old me. The other half distained the tacky television and newspaper folk who were blocking the pavement and spilling over into the street. All very ungodly.

The crowd was now augmented by some members of the English Heritage hierarchy and a few local dignitaries, all of whom fawned around the ageless pop star, leaving me out on the fringes. Because the party was in danger of causing a road accident, it was decided to abbreviate the proceedings, and so short speeches were called for. This meant that in essence I did little more than introduce Sir Cliff, who then described the noble actor in warm, personal terms that indicated they had been the closest of friends.

Cliff tugged the curtain cord and suddenly the plaque was exposed. The cameramen all wanted a snap of Cliff next to the inscription. This meant they had to go low and look up Cliff's nose, which he didn't seem to care for.

Quite abruptly the key players in the ceremony now hurried through the front door of the house for a few quiet drinks. I was signing an autograph for a *Flog It!* fan and so got cut off from the main party. As people dispersed, the front door of what had been John Mills's home was now firmly closed. I knocked hard, and after a moment the door was opened fractionally by a lofty toff, who told me this was a private function. He closed the door before I could explain who I was.

I knocked again but to no effect.

Raising a glass to Sir John Mills with Stanley Long.

Paul Martin's Britain

I'd been told the drinks were being served in the garden at the back, so I decided to make my way round. This proved complicated. From the side of the churchyard I could see the garden, but couldn't see how to reach it. I had the options of knocking on other front doors to ask permission to get through to the adjacent garden, or of climbing over a series of back garden fences. I took the latter course and scuttled across several lawns and flower beds before reaching the great and good of Denham.

Inside the house was a 1960s jukebox. I don't know if this had belonged to Sir John, but it contained a copy of Cliff's 'Lucky Lips'. Someone switched the machine on and Cliff cheerfully sang along to his ancient tune. You could see how he had sustained a place in showbiz. He had a great presence and warmth. I am mystified as to why he gets some stick in the papers. He's a Peter Pan who has never acted inappropriately in a fifty-year career. I guess others are jealous of him – for his talent, good humour and everlasting good looks.

I hoped the second part of the day might bring about an improvement to my status as a novice celebrity. I was due to help run a charity auction over lunch at Grosvenor House. Here I prayed I wouldn't have to climb over garden walls to reach the heart of the action. This time I made it into the reception area, where a woman immediately approached me.

'You're the *Flog It!* man, aren't you?'

'Yes, Paul Martin.'

'It's a great pleasure to meet you, Paul.'

'Thank you.'

It was Joan Sims and she asked me to call round some time and evaluate the objects she had collected from her *Carry On* film days.

But, best of all, a man approached me from the audience near the end and told me he was a big fan of me and my programme. It was one of my teenage heroes, Rick Wakeman.

A big thank you to everyone who has worked on *Flog It!* past and present. It's been a wonderful journey. Special thanks to Jay Hunt, my BBC1 and BBC2 controller, for championing my corner. And above all thank you to the millions of *Flog It!* fans who keep watching. As long as this keeps happening, I'll keep doing it, because I love it.

PICTURE CREDITS

The author and publisher are grateful for permission to reproduce the following images: *Bust Bara* (oil on canvas) by Norman Cornish (p. 104) is © University Gallery (painting) and Jim McAdam (photo); *Toil* (oil on canvas) by Mark Senior (1862–1927) (p. 105) is © Leeds Museums and Galleries (City Art Gallery) UK/The Bridgeman Art Library; *View into the Garden*, 1926 (oil on board), by Vanessa Bell (1879–1961) (p. 110) is © estate of Vanessa Bell, courtesy of Henrietta Garnett, and © Bolton Museum and Art Gallery, Lancashire, UK/The Bridgeman Art Library; *School is Out*, 1889, by Elizabeth Adela Stanhope Forbes (1859–1912) (p. 112) is © Penlee House Gallery and Museum, Penzance, Cornwall, UK/The Bridgeman Art Library; *The Rain it Raineth Every Day*, 1889, by Norman Garstin (1847–1926) (p. 113) is © Penlee House Gallery and Museum, Penzance, Cornwall, UK/The Bridgeman Art Library; the portrait of Dame Barbara Hepworth

(1903–75) seated in her garden next to one of her sculptures (p. 118) is © Photo Credit: Peter Kinnear/The Bridgeman Art Library; Hill Top, Sawrey (p. 128), is © NTPL/Joe Cornish; *Geese and Hoar-Frost* (watercolour on paper) by Charles Frederick Tunnicliffe (1901–79) (p. 135) is © Estate of Charles Frederick Tunnicliffe/Newport Museum and Art Gallery, South Wales/The Bridgeman Art Library; Glasgow School of Art, view of the exterior, built 1897–9, by Charles Rennie Mackintosh (1868–1928) (p. 146) is © Glasgow School of Art, Scotland/The Bridgeman Art Library; the oak sideboard by Sidney Barnsley, 1924 (p. 154), is © Cheltenham Art Gallery & Museums, Gloucestershire, UK/The Bridgeman Art Library; Croome Park, Worcestershire (p. 158), is © NTPL/David Noton; Stoney Road Allotments (p. 162) is © English Heritage.NMR; the photograph of SS *Great Britain* (p. 185) is © the estate of Mandy Reynolds ABIPP QEP; the photograph of the Bristol 410 (p. 193) is © Bristol Owners Club Heritage Trust; *Study for the Yellow Jockey* (oil on board) by Sir Alfred Munnings (1878–1959) (p. 207) is by courtesy of Felix Rosenstiel's Widow & Son Ltd, London © Sir Alfred Munnings Art Museum and © Private Collection/Roy Miles Fine Paintings/The Bridgeman Art Library.

The author and publisher are also grateful to the following: Phyllis Arnold, p. 139; Boo Beaumont, pp. 22, 29, 39; Andrew Garlick, p. 125; Stanley Long, pp. 236–8; Doug McKenzie, p. 243; National Railway Museum, pp. 41, 175; David Prentice, pp. 102–3; Stan Shaw, pp. 224, 226–7; Sutcliffe Gallery, pp. 170–1; Rosamund Wallinger, p. 123, and Liz Jones for various scenic shots.

Every effort has been made to trace the copyright holders of the images reproduced in this book. The author apologises if anyone's copyright has been accidentally infringed and can be contacted care of the Publisher.

ACKNOWLEDGEMENTS

My thanks to my literary agent, Mandy Little, of Watson, Little, and to all those who have been involved in the production of this book. In particular, a very big thank you to Mike Jackson (pictured above), BBC director, for factual research and on-the-road photography.